The World in the Buddhist Sense

Nina van Gorkom

2022

Published in April 2022 by:
Zolag
www.zolag.co.uk

ISBN 9781897633410
Copyright Nina van Gorkom

This work is licensed under the:
Creative Commons Attribution-NoDerivs 3.0 Unported License.
To view a copy of this license, visit:
http://creativecommons.org/licenses/by-nd/3.0/

Contents

1 Introduction   1

2 The World   9

3 Wrong view   19

4 Clear Comprehension   33

5 Nāma and rūpa   47

6 Direct experience   57

7 Concentration on Breathing   69

8 Mindfulness of breathing   85

9 Doing complicated things   97

10 Right awareness   109

11 Pāli Glossary   121

12 Books by Nina van Gorkom   135

1
Introduction

From our childhood we are used to the idea that this world we are living in with all the people around us is the real world. The Buddha taught that the world is composed of the objects which come to us through the senses of eyes, ears, nose, tongue, body-sense and through the door of the mind. These are all fleeting phenomena which change within split-seconds. Seeing is there just for a moment and then it falls away. Visible object is there just for a moment and then it falls away. What we used to take for our solid world consists of impermanent elements. Our world crumbles away, there is the disintegration of our world and of ourselves.

When the reader is in the first page of this book confronted with two different kinds of truths, the conventional truth and the absolute truth, he may wonder whether there is a discrepancy here which makes it impossible to practise Buddhism and at the same time to live one's life in the world. We have to do our work, to be with other people and we want to enjoy our possessions, all the things of this world. The Buddha did not deny that there is the conventional truth we have to live with. However, it is a great blessing that he taught us the absolute truth, the truth of mental phenomena, nāma, and physical phenomena, rūpa. Nāma and rūpa are terms in Pāli, the language in which the Buddhist scriptures have been written. We can develop understanding of the absolute truth, of nāma and rūpa, while we live our daily life naturally. Absolute truth is not a truth which cannot be grasped, it is not something abstract, it is the truth about daily realities. Understanding this truth will help us to be able to lead our life in the world in a more wholesome way and to face contrarieties in our work, and in our relationships.

How to develop understanding of nāma and rūpa naturally, while we are eating, doing our daily tasks, doing everything we normally do? This was the topic of the letters I wrote while living in Tokyo to someone who was wondering how to develop right understanding of nāma and rūpa in daily life. The Buddha taught mindfulness, in Pāli: sati, of the nāma and rūpa of our life, in order to acquire direct understanding of them. We discussed what sati is; it is difficult for all of us to understand this reality which seems so elusive. Sati is different from thinking, but what is it then? We have to accept that we cannot understand immediately what sati is, we have to study carefully all the phenomena of our life the Buddha taught. We need knowledge of them as a foundation. Gradually we can learn to investigate the nāmas and rūpas which appear in our life and then there can be conditions for direct awareness of them, for sati.

The reader may wonder what the purpose is of the study of nāma and rūpa. Why should one take so much trouble? It is important to have less ignorance about our life, about ourselves. The real cause of all our troubles is not the behaviour of other people or the situation we are in, but our own defilements. Our ignorance conditions many other defilements, such as selfishness, hatred, avarice and jealousy. Through the development of understanding there will be elimination of ignorance. When there is less ignorance it will be for the benefit of both ourselves and others. The development of understanding can only be very gradual. We need patience to investigate all phenomena which appear. At first we may believe that we know already what phenomena such as seeing, hearing or thinking are, but gradually it will dawn on us how ignorant we are of the most common phenomena of our life. That is the right beginning. We are hearing sounds the whole day, but what do we know about hearing? We may have thought that we can hear and define the sound or recognize what we hear all at the same time. Hearing is one moment, and knowing the meaning of what we hear such as the meaning of words are other moments. The reader may wonder why it is important to know this. It is important, because defilements arise immediately on account of what we experience through the senses. We ought to learn more about our defilements and the way they are conditioned. We hear pleasant and unpleasant sounds and after that, when we know the meaning and think about what was heard, we immediately react to it either in a negative way, or in a positive way. There may be unwholesome moments of clinging or aversion, or there may be wholesome moments of patience and wisdom. All this happens so quickly, within split-seconds, it is actually beyond control. When we investigate such processes in our life we can experience ourselves that there are many different nāmas which are beyond control. We cannot create our own hearing, nor can we direct the way we react, it has happened already when we realize it. The Buddha taught that nāma and rūpa arise because of their own conditioning factors. For example, when one reacts with patience to harsh sounds one can do so because it is in one's character to react in that way. Such inclination has already been accumulated. This is an example which illustrates that there is not one mind, but many different mental phenomena which change all the time.

We may wonder why we also have to learn about physical phenomena, rūpas. Is it necessary to learn so many details? Rūpas affect us very much all the time. We cling to pleasant rūpas and we dislike unpleasant rūpas. Through the ears the rūpa which is sound is experienced by hearing-consciousness. When we hear harsh words it is only sound which is heard, only the rūpa which impinges on the ear sense. However, we think with anger or sadness about an unkind person who spoke harsh words, we think in a negative, unwholesome way and this happens most of the time. In the absolute sense there is no person who speaks unkind words. The moments of consciousness which motivated his speaking are only fleeting moments, they have fallen away but we keep thinking about his unkindness. There is no person, no self who hears, hearing arises only for a moment and then it falls away. The sound which is heard is only a kind of rūpa which does not last. Right understanding of the objects we experience through the six doors will eventually lead to more patience. The effect will be that we are less inclined to feel hurt by what others say to us and that we will be able to forgive more easily.

The Buddha taught the impermanence of the phenomena of our life. We may believe that we know already that our body is subject to decay and that our thoughts and feelings change. We can think of impermanence but this is not the same as the direct knowledge of the changes from moment to moment of nāma and rūpa. A very precise knowledge of nāma and rūpa has to be developed so that later on their arising and falling away, their impermanence, can be directly experienced. When one has come to that stage there will be less enslavement to the objects one experiences. However, this is a learning process which has to continue for a long time, even longer than this life. There is no quick result, no shortcut.

The person who wrote to me wanted to create particular situations in order to have more mindfulness. He thought that concentration on breathing would help him to reach the goal sooner. In Letter 6 and 7, I deal with mindfulness of breathing. There are many misunderstandings about this subject. When one concentrates on breathing one may be able to eliminate worry for those moments, one cannot think of anything else when one thinks of breathing. However, there is right concentration and wrong concentration, as I tried to explain in these letters. When there is right concentration there is calm which is wholesome and when there is wrong concentration there is unwholesome consciousness. When one clings to a quick result there is wrong concentration. I deal with this subject and quote from the commentary, the Visuddhimagga, in order to show how complex this subject is. If one does not know precisely the way of development of mindfulness of breathing there is wrong concentration and this is useless. It is already a gain when one understands that mindfulness of breathing is not just sitting and trying to concentrate on breath without knowing anything.

The Buddha taught that nāma and rūpa are impermanent and not self. What we take for a person or a self are only fleeting elements. When we begin to develop understanding of nāma and rūpa we have not eliminated the idea of self. There is still another person who speaks harsh words to us, and there is still "self" who hears them and is angry. The fact that we think in this way is conditioned by remembrance of past experiences, we always thought in that way. Also thinking is a conditioned nāma, it is a reality. The person we think of is not an absolute reality but a conventional reality. We do not have to behave in an artificial way while we develop understanding of phenomena, but while we answer back to someone who speaks to us there can be a short moment in between of realising the truth that whatever we say or do is conditioned, that it is not "I". We are not used to such an approach, but gradually it can be learnt if we see its benefit. When we do not want to mislead ourselves about the fleeting phenomena of our life right understanding can begin to develop, it develops, there is no self who develops it. We may feel happy or sad, just as we used to, but in between understanding of such phenomena can very gradually be accumulated.

We can learn from our own experience the difference between the moments we are living in the world of conventional realities, the world of self, people and possessions, and the moments there is one nāma or rūpa appearing through one of the six doorways. We usually live with our illusions and dreams, we are led by the outward appearance of things and we are ignorant of what is really going on within us or around us. We look at our surroundings and at other people and we make our own mental pictures of what we observe. We are all different, with different inclinations, and this conditions the way we see the people and things around us. Each of us lives in his own world of thinking. We live most of the time in our own world of thinking, but through the study of the Buddha's teachings we begin to understand the difference between imaginations and realities.

The Buddha taught that there is no person, no self who can exert control over nāma and rūpa, they are beyond control. It may be difficult to accept this since we want to control our life. When there is seeing which experiences a pleasant visible object there is attachment to this object immediately. When there is seeing which experiences an unpleasant object there is aversion to this object immediately. The Buddha taught about realities in detail. A very precise knowledge of the different realities should be developed. Then we will find out that there are many more unwholesome moments, moments of attachment, aversion and ignorance, than we ever thought. These moments arise because of their own conditions but there can be the development of understanding of them. When understanding has been fully developed unwholesomeness can be eradicated, but that is a long way off. Even though the final goal is a long way off it is valuable to develop understanding. When there is a short moment of understanding we learn to see that there is only a nāma or only a rūpa, and consequently we will be less inclined to see them as very important. Understanding will condition more evenmindedness. Gradually we will learn to see nāma and rūpa as they are: impermanent and not self.

The reader may wonder why I use Pāli terms. The Buddhist teachings are contained in the Tipiṭaka, the three "Baskets" which are the Vinaya (the book of discipline for the monks), the Suttanta (discourses), and the Abhidhamma, which deals with absolute realities in detail. The Scriptures as they have come to us date from the Buddha's time, the sixth century B.C. and they are in the Pāli language. I have also quoted from the Visuddhimagga which is a summary of the teachings written by Buddhaghosa in the beginning of the fifth century A.D. In different English translations of the texts the Pāli terms have been rendered differently and thus confusion may arise as to which reality has been referred to by which term. The Buddha's teaching of realities is very precise and therefore it is useful to learn some of the Pāli terms which represent these realities. In the back of this book is a glossary to help the reader. The reader should not be discouraged by the Pāli terms. When one continues to study one will find that they are helpful for a more precise understanding of what the Buddha taught about all the different phenomena which occur right now.

The scriptures are deep in meaning and it is difficult to understand the application of the Buddha's teachings. Therefore I feel deep gratitude to Ms. Sujin in Thailand, who helped me to understand the Buddha's teachings and pointed to me the way to develop understanding of realities in daily life. Without such a good friend in Dhamma one will easily misunderstand the scriptures and apply them in the wrong way. I also wish to express my appreciation to the "Dhamma Study and Propagation Foundation" and to the publisher Alan Weller. Without their help the publication of this book would not have been possible.

While we study we should not forget the purpose of our study. The purpose is not theoretical knowledge, but direct understanding of our own life, of all our wholesome moments and unwholesome moments, all the nāmas and rūpas occurring at this moment. When we learn more about the conditions for these phenomena we will begin to see that they are beyond control, not self. The Buddha's message to us is to investigate the truth and to prove the truth through developing direct understanding, and this understanding can eradicate ignorance and all other defilements. May the reader investigate the truth himself!

Nina van Gorkom

2
The World

15 January
Tokyo
1971

Dear Mr. G.,

You asked me questions about mindfulness in daily life. You said that you can be aware while shaving, but that you are not yet sure about the experience of different characteristics of nāma (mental phenomena) and rūpa (physical phenomena). I would like to quote from the Kindred Sayings (IV, Saḷāyatana-vagga, Second Fifty, Chapter IV, §84, Transitory). We read that Ānanda asked the Buddha what the world is:

> "The world! The world!" is the saying, lord. Pray, how far, lord, does this saying go? What is transitory by nature, Ānanda, is called "the world" in the Ariyan discipline. And what, Ānanda, is transitory by nature? The eye, Ānanda, is transitory by nature... objects... tongue... mind is transitory by nature, mind-states, mind-consciousness, mind-contact, whatsoever pleasant feeling or unpleasant feeling or indifferent feeling arises owing to mind-contact, that also is transitory by nature. What is thus transitory, Ānanda, is called "the world" in the Ariyan discipline.

We cannot yet directly experience the impermanence of nāma and rūpa, but we will know the "world in the sense of the ariyan discipline" if we develop right understanding of absolute realities, paramattha dhammas, by being mindful of their characteristics as they appear one at a time through the six doorways.

We are used to thinking that there are the world of our work, of our home, of meditation, so many kinds of worlds. Actually we should consider what the realities are which can be directly experienced. These are the nāma and rūpa which appear through the six doors. There is seeing-consciousness, which experiences visible object through the eye-door. There is hearing-consciousness which experiences sound through the ear-door. There is smelling-consciousness which experiences odour through the nose. There is tasting-consciousness which experiences flavour through the tongue. There is body-consciousness which experiences tangible object through the body-door. There is mind-consciousness which experiences mind-objects through the mind-door. Thus, there are actually six worlds appearing through the six doors. It will take a long time to develop a clearer understanding of the six worlds. Thinking about them is not enough. In being mindful of different characteristics we will come to understand "the world in the sense of the ariyan discipline" through our own experience.

Coming back to your example of shaving, you notice different moments. Can you notice that there are different realities with different characteristics? When you look into the mirror, touch the razor, when you are thinking, could you simply, without any need to "detect" nāma and rūpa, just realize that these different moments are different experiences which have different characteristics? We should know that there are different realities. When you are looking into the mirror is there no seeing? It experiences just what appears through the eye-sense, visible object. When you close your eyes the reality which appeared when you were looking does not appear any more. Considering this is the first step to know what realities are. Later on one will learn more through direct experience.

You write that you experience "touching the razor". Which realities appear? Cold, motion or hardness? These are physical phenomena which can be experienced through touch. Or does a nāma appear which experiences one of these rūpas? Can you realize that they have different characteristics? This will help you to know the world in the ariyan sense.

When you eat breakfast you touch the fork. We call it "fork", but what can you directly experience through the body-sense? The rūpas which are cold, hardness or motion? You can learn that, no matter whether we touch a razor or a fork, rūpas such as cold, hardness or motion can be experienced through the body-sense. It is not you who experiences them, but only a type of nāma which experiences them. Through the eye-sense the rūpa which is visible object or colour can be experienced. The world of tangible object is different from the world appearing through the eye-sense. You might say, "But I experience the razor and the fork. I know when I touch the razor and when I touch the fork." How do you know what is a razor and what is a fork? Because of remembrance or perception, saññā, a mental factor, cetasika, which arises with every moment of consciousness, citta. There isn't any experience which is not accompanied by saññā. Because of saññā we remember things, we remember what different things are used for. We remember, "when we do this, it has that effect". Saññā is another reality, it is a kind of nāma, not self.

In the "absolute sense", or, in the "ariyan discipline", there is no fork, no razor, no mirror; these are only ideas we can think of, but they are not realities. When there is seeing, it is visible object which is experienced; when there is touching, it is hardness, coldness or another rūpa presenting itself through the body-sense, which is experienced. When we remember that we call a particular thing a "fork" or a "razor", or when we remember how to use them, the reality presenting itself at that moment is a kind of nāma. Realities are experienced through the six doorways, presenting themselves one at a time. They are not a person, not a thing which can stay, they are nāma and rūpa which arise and then fall away immediately. This is the truth which can be directly experienced, this is the "world" in the ariyan discipline.

Is this not more simple than you would have thought at first? There is thinking when you are shaving. Is that not different from seeing, from touching? Attachment or aversion may arise on account of what is experienced. Are these not realities different from seeing, from visible object, from the experience of tangible object or from the rūpas which are experienced through the body-sense? It would be helpful to realize that all these realities which appear are different, that they have different characteristics. They are nāma and rūpa which arise because of conditions, not self. We cling so much to concepts and ideas which we convey to others by means of conventional terms in language. We cling to saññā, we are infatuated with all the ideas and stories we remember, such as razor, fork, person. This blinds us to the world in the ariyan sense. It prevents us from understanding nāma and rūpa as they present themselves through the six doors, one at a time.

You wrote that you often wake up with mindfulness. I often wake up with attachment, lobha, or aversion, dosa. For example, I think, "What difficult thing do I have to do today?" Sometimes I have to hear unpleasant words from other people, and then I feel unhappy. Why? Because at those moments I do not see the world in the ariyan sense. When we hear unpleasant words, the hearing is only vipāka (citta which is result of kamma), it is nāma which arises just for a moment and then falls away immediately. When I have aversion, there is akusala citta (unwholesome consciousness), which is another kind of nāma. In the ariyan sense there is no "I"who experiences, there is no experiencer. There is not this or that person who says unpleasant words to me. There are only nāma and rūpa. There is seeing, hearing, thinking and other phenomena which appear for a moment and are then gone. There are different feelings arising because of different conditions. The teachings are very helpful for the understanding of our life. When we listen to the sutta texts we can be reminded to be aware of realities.

You find that there is more awareness when you do things which do not require so much attention, things which are done automatically, like shaving. You wrote "Shaving is there. It presents itself as if done by someone else."

"Shaving is there", these are words you use to describe a whole situation you can think of, but which are the realities you can directly experience? There is the world in the ariyan sense: different phenomena presenting themselves through the six doors. Seeing, touching or thinking are realities, but shaving is not a reality. "Shaving presents itself as if done by someone else". What is this? It is a thought, that is all. We should not cling to special sensations, they are only nāmas which do not stay. Thinking is only one kind of reality which appears, and then there are other realities.

Is it true that there is more awareness when we do things

which do not require much attention? At the Japanese school I have to be attentive to the teacher who asks me questions in Japanese which I have to answer, applying the grammar I learnt. We should not exclude beforehand the arising of awareness in such situations. If there can be awareness sometimes of different realities one can begin to develop understanding of them. Mindfulness arises when there are conditions for its arising and we cannot say beforehand, "In such circumstances it will arise, in such circumstances it will not arise". Awareness is anattā, not self. We may think that it cannot arise in particular circumstances, but this is only our thinking. We should realize such a moment of thinking as only a kind of nāma which arises because of conditions.

Sati, mindfulness, of the Eightfold Path will not arise often when it has not been accumulated enough yet. We may take for mindfulness what is actually only a sensation of quietness and "some notion of what is going on", as you write. But this is not knowing a characteristic of a reality which appears through one of the six doors, it is merely pondering at leisure.

When hardness is experienced through touch we may take for sati what is actually attachment. Do we wish to have many moments of sati? Then we are clinging and right understanding cannot develop. Our aim should be to learn more about the realities which appear one at a time. We cling to visible object, sound and all the other sense objects. We may not notice it that we cling to them, but is it not true that we are usually absorbed by these objects and think about them for a long time? We think that we see people and different things, but we can learn that what appears through eyes is only visible object. We think that we hear the voice of someone, but what appears through the ears is only sound, there is no person in the sound. We can learn to consider the phenomena of our daily life as only different realities which appear one at a time.

There can be "study" of visible object, sound, hearing and

other realities when they appear one at a time. The word "study" is appropriate, because it is a learning process. It is not theoretical study but study of nāma and rūpa in daily life. We should not have expectations about the arising of clear, direct understanding of nāma and rūpa. When there are expectations there is attachment to an idea of self who is successful, whereas mindfulness and right understanding should lead to detachment from the idea of self. We should remember that mindfulness of nāma and rūpa accompanies kusala citta and that kusala citta does not arise as often as akusala citta. There are countless more moments of akusala citta than kusala citta. If we remember this we will be less inclined to false expectations. When we have understood that there should be study of the characteristics of nāma and rūpa in order to have more understanding of them, we will stop wondering what mindfulness is or doubting about it.

There is usually forgetfulness of nāma and rūpa, but sometimes there can be kusala citta accompanied by mindfulness of the reality which appears at the present moment, a nāma or a rūpa. We cannot do anything special to cause the arising of sati because sati is anattā. It arises because of its appropriate conditions. The right conditions for sati are: listening to the Dhamma, theoretical understanding of nāma and rūpa and deeply considering the Dhamma in our life. One may be discouraged about it that, although one has listened for many years, there is hardly any awareness in daily life. When one merely listens but does not deeply consider what one heard and does not test the meaning of it, there are no conditions for awareness. Through considering the Dhamma one builds up one's own understanding, one is not dependent on other people. Everybody should consider nāma and rūpa in his own situation.

You asked in your letter what the difference is between sati and thinking. There can be thinking with kusala citta and with akusala citta. Most of the time there is thinking with clinging or with aversion. When there is thinking in the right way about nāma and rūpa it can condition right awareness later on, but we do not know when. When we think about sati we will not know its characteristic, but when right mindfulness of nāma and rūpa arises we will know what sati is. We can notice that there are countless moments of thinking in a day, and when there is thinking it is time to study the characteristic of thinking. Then we can come to know it as a nāma which arises because of its own conditions, not self. It is the thinking which thinks.

"Sometimes sati seems to be contemporaneous with its object, sometimes later", you write. We should be careful and not mistake thinking for sati. When there is study with awareness of one reality at a time, the reality which appears, one does not think about sati as being contemporaneous with its object or not. There is at that moment only the characteristic of the nāma or rūpa which appears.

You want to know when in the process of cittas sati arises. Sati has to accompany kusala citta, but it can be mindful also of akusala citta. When for example aversion, dosa, arises, it can be object of mindfulness. Cittas succeed one another very rapidly and after the dosa has fallen away there can be in another process kusala cittas with sati. Sati can then be mindful of the dosa which has fallen away. If there is unpleasant feeling now can there not be study of its characteristic, in order to know it as not self, not my unpleasant feeling? We are inclined to take feeling for self, but when we understand that feelings arise because of conditions we will be less inclined to take them for mine or self. Sometimes I take things to heart and I have unpleasant feeling, sometimes not. This is because of different conditions. We should learn that there is no self who can control feelings. We do not have to think of processes when there is the study of different characteristics. All that matters is to know the world in the ariyan sense. This world is a new world to us since we used to know only the world of conventional truth, the world of self, people and possessions. When there is no development of understanding of nāma and rūpa, akusala cittas will arise very often: we are infatuated with the objects we experience, we have aversion towards them or there is ignorance about realities. When we, for example, see a teapot, we may be ignorant of the six worlds in the ariyan sense. When we are confused as to the different doorways, we think that what presents itself through the eye-door is a teapot and we take it for something which stays. However, through the eye-door it is only visible object that presents itself, just for a moment. When we touch the teapot, the rūpas which are hardness, softness, heat or cold may present themselves. In order to know realities as they are we should be aware of them as they present themselves through the different doorways, one at a time. Like and dislike are again different phenomena and we should not confuse them with seeing or visible object. Thinking of the concept "teapot" is again another reality, a type of nāma. Whatever nāma or rūpa appears can be object of mindfulness and thus right understanding can develop. If there is preference for particular types of nāma or rūpa which seem to be so clear, there is clinging. We should learn different characteristics of nāma and rūpa as we go along in daily life; when walking, standing, getting up, taking a bath, eating, listening or talking. Only thus will there be the disintegration of the "self ". We will know the world in the ariyan sense. We read in the Kindred Sayings (IV, Saḷāyatana-vagga, Kindred Sayings on Sense, Third Fifty, Chapter IV, §136) that the Buddha said to the monks:

> Devas and mankind, monks, delight in objects, they are excited by objects. It is owing to the instability, the coming to an end, the ceasing of objects, monks, that devas and mankind live woefully. They delight in sounds, scents, savours, in touch, they delight in mind-states, and are excited by them. It

is owing to the instability, the coming to an end, the ceasing of mind-states, monks, that devas and mankind live woefully.

But the Tathāgata, monks, who is arahat, a Fully-enlightened One, seeing, as they really are, both the arising and the destruction, the satisfaction, the misery and the way of escape from objects,—he delights not in objects, takes not pleasure in them, is not excited by them. It is owing to the instability, the coming to an end, the ceasing of objects that the Tathāgata dwells at ease.

Is this real life or not? When we do not see things as they are we are enslaved. How did the Buddha become free? By fully knowing realities, by knowing their characteristics as they appear through the six doors.

With mettā

Nina van Gorkom

3

Wrong view

Tokyo
15 February
1971

Dear Mr. G.,

First I will quote your question about personality-belief: "I wish you could tell me more about personality-belief, sakkāya-diṭṭhi. Is sakkāya-diṭṭhi. wrong view? But, if I have wrong view, it is only a kind of nāma, to be recognized as such." Sakkāya is a name for the five khandhas which are objects of clinging. Sakkāya-diṭṭhi is wrong view about the five khandhas. We have accumulated wrong view about them during many lives. There is wrong view about the khandhas when we really believe that

CHAPTER 3. WRONG VIEW

they are permanent and self.

All conditioned realities in ourselves and around ourselves can be classified as five khandhas and these are the following:

rūpa-kkhandha physical phenomena

vedanā-kkhandha feelings

saññā-kkhandha remembrance

saṅkhāra-kkhandha cetasikas (mental factors) except feeling and saññā

viññāṅa-kkhandha all cittas

This classification may seem rather theoretical, but it is a classification of realities which arise now. There are the five khandhas now while you are seeing. There is the eye-sense which is rūpa-kkhandha, there is visible object which is also rūpa-kkhandha, there is seeing which is viññāṇa-kkhandha. Seeing is accompanied by feeling, vedanā-kkhandha, by remembrance, saññā-kkhandha, and by other cetasikas which are saṅkhāra-kkhandha. The khandhas arise and fall away, they do not stay and none of the khandhas is self. Do you have an idea of a self who is seeing? It is only viññāṇa-kkhandha which arises for an extremely short moment, performs the function of seeing and then falls away. Seeing arises because of its own conditions. eye-sense and visible object are conditions for seeing. Without these conditions you could not see. Can you create your own eye-sense? It arises because of its appropriate conditions. Seeing, eye-sense and visible object do not belong to you. Do you think that you see people? It is only visible object, rūpa-kkhandha, which is seen just for a moment and then falls away.

When we have listened to the Dhamma we understand in theory that there is no self, no being, but our understanding is still weak. We do not directly experience the truth of realities as they appear one at a time. We cling to the khandhas and have an idea that they can last. Do we have a notion of a "whole" of mind and body, of "my personality"? What we take for a whole of mind and body are only five khandhas which arise and fall away. We also cling to rūpas outside ourselves and consider them as things which last. Don't we cling to our possessions, to our house and all the things in it? We may be stingy, we may not be inclined to give things away. We should remember that what we take for our possessions are only rūpa-kkhandha which arises and falls away.

There is not necessarily wrong view every time we cling to the khandhas. We may just be attached to our body without there being wrong view about it. We can cling to the khandhas with conceit. When we have conceit and compare our body or our mental qualities with those of someone else there cannot be wrong view at the same time. Conceit and wrong view cannot arise together. We learn from the Abhidhamma that there are eight different types of lobha-mūla-cittas, cittas which are rooted in attachment, of which four are accompanied by wrong view, diṭṭhi, and four unaccompanied by wrong view. When one has studied the Dhamma and acquired intellectual understanding about the nature of not self of realities it does not mean that one has realized the truth of not self. We have accumulated so much ignorance about realities and the latent tendency of wrong view has not been eradicated. Only the sotāpanna who has developed understanding to the degree that enlightenment could be realized has eradicated the latent tendency to wrong view. Paññā, right understanding, must be developed in order to realize nāma and rūpa as impermanent and not self.

You wrote to me that when you have wrong view it can be recognized as such. It is not easy to know exactly when there is clinging with wrong view and when without wrong view. Only when paññā is keener it can know the different characteristics of realities more clearly.

We are so used to thinking that we see people, houses and trees. Do we really study with awareness seeing which appears now or visible object which appears now? Do we study again and again the realities which appear one at a time? Only in that way can we find out that no person can appear through the eyes but only visible object, that which is visible. We prefer to think about people and things, we prefer to live in the world of our thoughts instead of studying realities such as seeing or visible object. We have accumulated the tendency to be absorbed in our thoughts about people and things, and thus it is natural that we are inclined to thinking about those things which are not real, which are only concepts or ideas. It is not self who thinks, but a type of nāma which arises because of its own conditions. We should not try to push away our thinking but we can begin to notice the difference between the moments we are absorbed in our thoughts and the moments of being aware of one reality at a time, such as visible object or seeing. In this way we can learn the difference between concepts or ideas and realities. Only when we know the difference we can gradually learn how to study realities with awareness and in this way there can be more understanding of them.

You have asked me what it means to take something for "self", for "attā ".

Attā or self implies something which stays. Where is the self, does it have a characteristic which can be directly experienced? Is the body the self? The body consists of rūpas which arise and then fall away immediately. Is feeling self? Feelings change all the time, they can be happy, unhappy or indifferent. Is thinking self? Thinking changes all the time, thus, how could you identify yourself with thinking? When we learn to be aware of the phenomena which appear through the six doors we will lose interest in things which cannot be directly experienced but which are only objects of speculation.

Even though we may not expressively think, "It is I", we are likely to be confused about realities. So long as right understanding has not been developed we join different realities together into a "mass", a "whole". For example, we do not distinguish the characteristic of sound from the characteristic of hearing, and thus our knowledge of them is still vague. We do not distinguish hearing from thinking about what we heard, or from like and dislike. When understanding has not been developed yet we are also confused as to the different doorways through which objects are experienced. For example, hearing experiences sound through the ear-door and thinking about what was heard experiences its object through the mind-door.

You asked me what the difference is between seeing a rose and seeing its colour.

There is seeing time and again but there is no right understanding of it. We do not realize the characteristics of phenomena as they appear one at a time through the different doorways. The nāma which sees only experiences visible object or colour through the eye-door. When we recognize an object such as a rose there is not seeing. The object is not colour but a concept or idea we form up by thinking. The thinking of the concept "rose" is conditioned by seeing but seeing and thinking arise at different moments. There is the experience of colour and there is thinking of the concept rose, and then colour impinges again on the eye-door and there is seeing again. How fast cittas change, how fast objects change! In which world do we mostly live? Do we know the six worlds appearing through the six doors or do we live only in the world of conventional truth? Is it wisdom to know only one world? Should we not know the worlds appearing through the six doors by being aware of different characteristics? In that way the self can gradually be broken up into elements until there is nothing left of it.

We will keep on clinging to the "whole" of the five khandhas, to body and mental phenomena so long as we have not realized that they are only elements which do not stay. We read in the

CHAPTER 3. WRONG VIEW

Kindred Sayings (III, Khandhā-vagga, Kindred Sayings on Elements, Middle Fifty, Chapter 5, §102, Impermanence) that the Buddha said to the monks at Sāvatthī:

> The perceiving of impermanence, monks, if practised and enlarged, wears out all sensual lust, all lust of rebirth, all ignorance, it wears out, tears out all conceit of "I am".
>
> Just as, monks, in the autumn season a ploughman with a great ploughshare, cuts through the spreading roots as he ploughs; even so, monks, the perceiving of impermanence, if practised and enlarged, wears out all sensual lust, wears out all lust for body, all lust for rebirth, wears out all ignorance, wears out, tears out all conceit of "I am".

The Buddha uses several similes in order to explain that the perception of impermanence wears out all clinging, ignorance and conceit. Further on we read:

> Just as, monks, in the autumn season, when the sky is opened up and cleared of clouds, the sun, leaping up into the firmament, drives away all darkness from the heavens, and shines and burns and flashes forth; even so, monks, the perceiving of impermanence, if practised and enlarged, wears out all sensual lust, wears out all lust for body, all desire for rebirth, all ignorance, wears out, tears out all conceit of "I am". And in what way, monks, does it so wear them out? It is by seeing: "Such is body; such is the arising of body; such is the ceasing of body. Such is feeling, remembrance, the activities (saṅkhāra-kkhandha), such is consciousness, its arising and its ceasing."

Even thus practised and enlarged, monks, does the perceiving of impermanence wear out all sensual lust, all lust for body, all desire for rebirth, all ignorance, wears out, tears out all conceit of "I am".

When one begins to develop right understanding of nāma and rūpa there cannot yet be the direct realization of their arising and falling away. First their different characteristics have to be clearly known, nāma has to be known as nāma, different from rūpa, and rūpa has to be known as rūpa, different from nāma. Understanding develops stage by stage and it is at a later stage that the arising and falling away of the reality which appears can be directly known. However, even the sotāpanna who has realized nāma and rūpa as they are, as not self, has not eradicated all clinging and ignorance. Only the arahat has eradicated all kinds of clinging, all ignorance and conceit. When we read this sutta we can be reminded to begin to study with awareness the nāma and rūpa which appear now. Since it is a long way to realize their impermanence we should not delay the development of understanding of them.

You were wondering how there can be different characters of people, a "personality", if there is no self. There are accumulations, tendencies which are accumulated in the citta. Cittas arise and fall away but the citta which falls away conditions the next citta and that is why accumulations can be "carried on" from one citta to the next one. That is why we can notice that people have different inclinations, that they behave in different ways. Our behaviour is conditioned, it is not self. We cling to our personality, to the image we have of ourselves. We want to be good, we cling to our good deeds. We have not realized that there is no self, no matter kusala citta or akusala citta arises. We do not possess kusala, it cannot stay. It only arises for a moment and then akusala citta is bound to arise. Because of our ignorance we do not even notice when there is kusala citta and when akusala citta. For example, when we give something away with generosity there are kusala cittas which can be accompanied by pleasant feeling. Very shortly afterwards akusala cittas with attachment may arise and these can also be accompanied by pleasant feeling. We may, for instance, think," I did this very well; I have really achieved something; I did this." If there is no awareness we do not know the different moments of citta and the different moments of feeling. It seems that there is only one kind of feeling, pleasant feeling, which lasts, and it seems that it is kusala all the time. Thus we take for wholesome what is unwholesome. It is essential to have right understanding of kusala and akusala, otherwise kusala cannot be developed.

You wrote that you can be aware of more than one reality at a time. This is not possible. Each citta can have only one object at a time and thus also the citta with awareness can have only one object at a time. One may take for awareness what is only thinking. For example, one may have an idea of oneself seeing and hearing at the same time. Then there is thinking of a concept, of a "whole" of different phenomena which are joined together. If there can be awareness of different characteristics of realities which present themselves one at a time one will find out that awareness can be aware of only one object at a time. It is unpredictable which reality will present itself at which moment. It can be softness or hardness which impinges on the body-sense, it can be sound, visible object or another reality. So long as we do not distinguish between different realities which arise closely one after the other we will keep on thinking that realities last. For example, cittas with attachment may arise and then there may be thinking of the attachment. We may think with aversion about the attachment which arose a moment ago. If there can be awareness of different characteristics it can be known that attachment is one kind of reality and thinking with aversion another kind of reality. They arise because of their own conditions, they are beyond control, not self.

You asked me whether awareness of sound means recognizing sound as sound.

Who is recognizing sound as sound? Is there an idea of self who recognizes sound as sound? When two people say that they recognize sound as sound one person may have right understanding and the other person may not. We may understand in theory that sati is not self but we may still cling to an idea of "my sati". When one has desire for sati and one wants to create conditions for its arising one has not understood that sati is not self, that it arises because of its own conditions. One may imagine what sati should be like but instead of speculation about it one should keep in mind that the realities which appear and thus also sati and paññā are only conditioned phenomena which are beyond control. Beyond control means that they are not self. Our goal should not be to have many moments of sati but to develop right understanding of the nāma and rūpa which appear now. Sound appears time and again. Right understanding of sound can be developed when it appears and we do not need to think about sati. One may say that one recognizes sound as sound but one may not realize it as a kind of rūpa which appears through the ear-sense. One may name it "rūpa," but naming a reality is not the same as directly knowing its characteristic when it appears. In the beginning there cannot be a precise knowledge of nāma and rūpa but we should remember that it can be developed only when there is study with awareness of the nāma or rūpa presenting itself now.

You said that you can experience "something" of impermanence, "fluctuations" of phenomena. Then there is only thinking about an idea one has of impermanence. The arising and falling away of one nāma or rūpa at a time can, as I said, only be realized later on. It cannot be realized so long as one is still confused about the difference between nāma and rūpa. We live most of the time in the world of conventional truth, and there is much ignorance about the world of absolute truth, the world of paramattha dhammas. In your letter you give an example of young people who are displeased with situations in their countries and who commit acts of violence (dosa) in order to show that they are discontented. Their accumulated violence is the real cause that they commit these acts, and the situations they are displeased with are only opportunities for their accumulated dosa to appear. Dosa will always arise so long as it has not been eradicated.

In our daily life there are many moments of aversion, dosa. We may wake up with a slightly unpleasant feeling. At first we do not realize that there is dosa, but then we may remember an unpleasant event, for example, unkind words someone may have spoken to us the day before. Or we may worry about a difficult situation we will have to face that day. These circumstances are not the real cause of our dosa. The outward circumstances, the people we meet change, but there is still our accumulated dosa and it will come out, always finding an object. There will always be reasons for dosa so long as it has not been eradicated yet. The person who has attained the third stage of enlightenment, the anāgāmī, has eradicated dosa. The way leading to the eradication of defilements is the development of right understanding of them when they appear. There is no other way. How can we realize that dosa is a conditioned nāma? Not by thinking about the dosa which has fallen away already, or about the events which conditioned its arising, but by being aware of it when it appears at the present moment. Only if there is mindfulness of phenomena as they appear through the six doors will we gradually realize that they are conditioned realities, not self. If there is awareness only of phenomena appearing through the eye-door or through the ear-door, it is not enough. There is not only visible object or sound, but also seeing, hearing, attachment, lobha, aversion, dosa, and other realities. There can also be awareness of the different kinds of feelings which arise. Our feelings change all the time. There are feelings arising on account of what is seen, heard, smelt, tasted, of what is experienced through the body-sense and of what is thought. At each moment of citta the condition for the accompanying feeling changes and thus feelings change all the time. It does not appear to us this way when we cling to the feeling which has fallen away already. It exists no more but we keep on pondering over it. If we cling to feelings of the past, we live more in the world of illusions than in the world of realities, of paramattha dhammas.

In the Visuddhimagga (XX, 96) nāma and rūpa which arise and fall away are compared to the sound of a lute which arises because of conditions and falls away again. The text states:

> '...But just as there is no store, prior to its arising, of the sound that arises when a lute is played, nor does it come from any store when it arises, nor does it go in any direction when it ceases, nor does it persist as a store when it has ceased, but on the contrary, not having been, it is brought into being owing to the lute, the lute's neck, and the man's appropriate effort, and having been, it vanishes–so too all material and immaterial states, not having been, are brought into being, having been they vanish.'

It is beneficial to be reminded that the nāmas and rūpas which appear in our daily life arise because of conditions and then fall away. If we consider this thoroughly there will be less inclination to keep on thinking about what is past already. In this way there will be less forgetfulness of what appears now. You don't have to do anything special to be aware, there are objects impinging on the six doors time and again. When you touch water which is too hot heat presents itself. You may think, "This water is too hot", and then there is thinking. Hot water is a concept we think of, but heat is a reality, a rūpa, which impinges on the body-sense, it can be directly experienced. The rūpa which is heat, the nāma which experiences heat or the painful feeling can appear again and again, in between the thinking. These are all different phenomena which do not stay, which are not self. There is no person who has painful feeling, there is a nāma which feels. Painful feeling arises because of its own conditions. When there are not the right conditions for it it cannot arise.

When we hear harsh words there are conditions for unpleasant feeling, but there can also be moments of awareness in between. Besides unpleasant feeling there are sound, hearing and other realities appearing. In this way we can realize that unpleasant feeling is only one phenomenon among many other realities which each arise because of their own conditions. Whereas if we are not mindful we think that there is only "my unpleasant feeling" which seems to last. We may believe that this particular person, this place and this situation are the causes of our unhappiness. However, these are not the real causes. The real cause is our accumulated dosa.

When we are aware of nāma and rūpa there is less enslavement to the objects we experience. When there is awareness of visible object which appears through the eyes there is no enslavement to visible object. When there is awareness of sound which appears through the ears there is no enslavement to sound, and it is the same with regard to the objects which present themselves through the other doorways. Wisdom can make us free, but we should not expect results within a short time. Do you remember the sutta about the handle of the knife which wears out very slowly, in the Kindred Sayings (III, Khandhā-vagga, Middle Fifty, Adze-handle)? The Buddha speaks about the handle of a knife which one holds each day. It gradually wears away, but one cannot notice how much is worn out each day. We cannot control the frequency of awareness, since it is anattā, not self, arising because of its own conditions. However, even a few moments of awareness in between lobha, dosa and moha is very beneficial. One begins to develop the Path which will surely lead to freedom. We read about the condition for freedom from defilements in the Kindred Sayings (IV, Saḷāyatana-vagga, Kindred Sayings on Sense, Third Fifty, Chapter III; §124). We read about a conversation the housefather Ugga had with the Buddha:

> 'Pray, lord, what is the condition, what is the cause whereby in this world some beings are not wholly set free in this very life, while other beings are wholly set free?' 'There are, housefather, objects cognizable by the eye. sounds cognizable by the ear... scents... savours... tangibles cognizable by the body... mind-states cognizable by the mind... If he has grasping for them, housefather, a monk is not wholly set free. That, housefather, is the condition, that is the cause whereby in this world some beings are not wholly set free in this very life.
>
> Likewise, housefather, there are objects cognizable by the eye... If he has no grasping for them a monk is wholly set free. That, housefather, is the condition, that is the cause whereby in this very life some beings are not wholly set free, while other beings are wholly set free.'

When there is seeing, hearing, smelling, tasting, touching or thinking, are we free? Don't you find that at the moment of mindfulness of one object at a time there is a beginning of freedom? There is less enslavement to objects and one is on the way leading to the eradication of the wrong view of self, of "personality belief". There is no other way but the development of understanding of the realities which present themselves through eyes, ears, nose, tongue, body-sense and mind-door.

With mettā,

Nina van Gorkom

4

Clear Comprehension

Tokyo
1 March
1971

Dear Mr. G.,

"What is sati-sampajañña, clear comprehension? I am puzzled by this term." This was a question you asked me. There are many degrees of comprehension. What would "clear comprehension" mean, theoretical knowledge or the knowledge through one's own experience? Which would be clearer? Does the sotāpanna have clear comprehension of nāmas and rūpas, of the world in the ariyan sense? Is the degree of clear comprehension of the arahat still higher? What is the way to develop clear comprehension, is it through thinking about realities or through awareness of them when they present themselves? Would awareness of realities not be the way that comprehension becomes clearer in different stages?

The term sati-sampajañña is composed of the word sati, mindfulness or awareness, and the word sampajañña which means discrimination or comprehension. The commentary to the Dialogues of the Buddha (Dīgha Nikāya), the Sumaṅgalavilāsinī, explains that there is a fourfold sampajañña. These aspects make it clear that there are different levels of sati-sampajañña. They are the following kinds of sati-sampajañña:

1. sātthaka-sampajañña: comprehension with regard to the purpose

2. sappāya-sampajañña: comprehension of what is suitable, fitting

3. gocara-sampajañña: comprehension of the object

4. asammoha-sampajañña: comprehension of non-delusion

Sātthaka-sampajañña, comprehension with regard to the purpose, pertains to our bodily health as well as to the growth of kusala and understanding. The Buddha was considerate of the monk's bodily and mental welfare. The monk was taught to have comprehension of the purpose with regard to the taking of alms food and the use of the other requisites. There are rules for the monks with regard to the use of them. He should not use them with attachment. We read in the Visuddhimagga (I, 85) about the way he should use alms food:

'Reflecting wisely, he uses alms food neither for amusement nor for intoxication nor for smartening nor for embellishment, but only for the endurance and continuance of this body, for the ending of discomfort, and for assisting the life of purity: "Thus I shall put a stop to old feelings and shall not arouse new feelings, and I shall be healthy and blameless and live in comfort." '

The monk will use alms food just as a sick man uses medicine. He will put a stop to the feeling of hunger and he will not indulge in immoderate eating.

The Buddha, on the day of his enlightenment, stopped fasting and he took the rice-gruel which was offered to him by Sujātā. He had understood that the undertaking of severe ascetical practices was not the Middle Way.

Also laypeople can apply to a certain extent, in their own situation, some of the rules of training for the monks. When there is sati-sampajañña while we are eating, it knows the right purpose of the taking of food. We do not have to think all the time what the purpose is of what we are doing. When sati-sampajañña arises it knows the right purpose. When there is clear comprehension with regard to the purpose of the taking of food, there are conditions not to indulge in food, but to take it as a medicine for the body. One can find out what is right for one's health. One should not torture oneself by staying too long in one position of the body. Some people have desire for tranquillity and they are hoping to be able to develop it to a high degree by sitting for a long time. When there is clear comprehension with regard to the purpose one will not torture oneself, one will stretch at the right time or change one's posture.

Sati-sampajañña with regard to the purpose is necessary for the development of kusala and right understanding. When we visit the good friend in Dhamma who explains the Dhamma in the right way, or when we visit the holy places in India it can be done with sati-sampajañña with regard to the purpose, namely the development of right understanding. We read in the Gradual Sayings (Book of the Tens, Chapter XVIII, §4) about aim and not-aim. The Buddha said to the monks:

'And what, monks, is not aim? Taking life, taking

what is not given, wrong conduct in sexual desires, falsehood, slander, bitter speech, idle babble, coveting, harmfulness and wrong view. This, monks, is called not-aim.'

We then read that the abstaining from akusala kamma is aim. Sati-sampajañña with regard to the purpose sees the benefit of kusala and the disadvantage of akusala. When other people speak in a harsh way to us we think immediately of ourselves, of our own interest. What is really useful to ourselves? When sati-sampajañña arises it sees the benefit of patience and lovingkindness, it sees the benefit of all kinds of kusala. When other people are unkind they give us an opportunity to cultivate patience and endurance. We need sati-sampajañña with regard to the purpose in daily life. If one wants to develop calm (samatha) one needs sati-sampajañña which knows the benefit of kusala and which sees the disadvantage of attachment to the sense objects. When one has desire for tranquillity the citta is akusala, but one may not notice it. In order to develop calm which is wholesome there must be sati-sampajañña which realizes the disadvantage of desire. So long as there is desire one will not reach the goal.

For the development of the Eightfold Path sati-sampajañña with regard to the aim is necessary. We read in the Gradual Sayings (Book of the Tens, Chapter XIV, §4) that the Buddha said to the monks that the factors of the wrong path are not-aim. As regards aim, we read:

'And what, monks, is aim? Right view, right thinking, right speech, right action, right effort, right mindfulness, right concentration, right knowledge and right release...'

When one follows the wrong path there is no sati-sampajañña. When one develops the right path there is clear comprehension with regard to the aim. The goal is the eradication of wrong view and all the other defilements. If one develops the right path one will eventually reach the goal.

We believe that right understanding of nāma and rūpa is what we value most highly in life, but is this true? We should be sincere and get to know our own accumulations. Don't we find our work and our relaxation more important than the development of right understanding? If there is sati-sampajañña which sees the value of awareness of realities right understanding can develop during the time we are working and also during the time of relaxation. There are nāma and rūpa all the time, no-matter where we are. There can be a beginning of the study of them when they appear. We do not have to go to a quiet place and change our usual way of life in order to develop understanding. When there is desire for awareness it will hinder the development of understanding of our life, of our accumulations. We have accumulated attachment to pleasant things, we like to go to concerts or watch T.V. We should learn to see that in such situations there are only dhammas, realities, which arise because of their own conditions. If we do not get to know lobha as it is, as only a conditioned reality, enlightenment cannot be attained and defilements cannot be eradicated.

The second sampajañña, sappāya-sampajañña, is knowing what is suitable, fitting to oneself. This sampajañña appertains to our bodily health as well as to the development of kusala. We know that we should not neglect our bodily health and therefore we should know what is suitable for us in order to avoid sickness and to live in comfort. We should find out, for example, what is the right kind of food for us and what not. What is suitable for one person may not be suitable for another person. We need sappāya-sampajañña in order to know the right conditions for our bodily health. We also need sappāya-sampajañña in order to know the right conditions for the development of kusala. Those who have accumulations to develop samatha should know the particular conditions which have to be fulfilled in order to develop calm. Most important is right understanding which knows precisely when the citta is kusala and when akusala, otherwise calm cannot be developed. Sappāya-sampajañña is needed in order to know which of the meditation subjects is suitable to oneself so that calm can grow. The meditation on corpses, for example, is not suitable for everybody, for some people this subject conditions aversion or fear. If one has accumulations to develop calm to the degree of jhāna one has to live in a secluded place. One needs sappāya-sampajañña in order to find out which place is suitable to oneself.

For the development of vipassanā the conditions are different from the conditions for the development of calm. The conditions for the development of vipassanā are: association with the right friend who can explain the Dhamma, listening, considering and testing the meaning of what one has heard. In this way there can be the correct understanding of the Eightfold Path. If there is sappāya-sampajañña which knows what is suitable for the development of right understanding it will develop.

We read in the Kindred Sayings (IV, Kindred Sayings on Sense, Saḷāyatana-vagga, Third Fifty, Chapter V, §146, Helpful) about the "sappāya" which leads to that which should be valued most highly: the eradication of defilements. This "sappāya", this helpful condition, is the perception of impermanence. We read that the Buddha said to the monks:

> 'I will teach you, monks, a way that is helpful for Nibbāna. Do you listen to it. And what, monks, is that way?
>
> Herein, monks, a monk regards the eye as impermanent. He regards visible object, eye-consciousness, eye-contact, as impermanent. That pleasant or unpleasant or indifferent feeling which arises by eye-contact–that also he regards as impermanent.

He regards the ear... the nose... the tongue, savours, tongue-consciousness, tongue-contact as impermanent. That pleasant or unpleasant or indifferent feeling, which arises by tongue-contact–that also he regards as impermanent.

He regards the body... he regards the mind, mind-states, mind-consciousness, mind-contact as impermanent. The pleasant or unpleasant or indifferent feeling... arising therefrom–he regards that also as impermanent.

This, monks, is the way that is helpful for Nibbāna.'

The impermanence of the realities which appear through the six doors cannot be realized immediately. First the rūpa which appears has to be realized as rūpa and the nāma which appears has to be realized as nāma. Their arising and falling away cannot be realized if one cannot clearly discern their different characteristics. This sutta reminds us to at least begin with awareness of realities such as visible object, seeing, feeling or attachment, of the realities which appear now. That is the condition which is helpful to gain more understanding.

The third sampajañña is gocara-sampajañña. Gocara literally means place or domain. In this case it is not the place where one should stay but "where citta goes", the object, ārammaṇa, of the citta. When gocara-sampajañña arises there is comprehension of the object of mindfulness. All realities which appear now through the six doors are the gocara or "domain" of sati of the Eightfold Path. All of the nāmas and the rūpas are included in the four "satipaṭṭhāna", the applications of mindfulness. They are: mindfulness of the body, of feeling, of citta and of dhammas. The object of sati is a paramattha dhamma which appears now, it is not a concept such as a body, a hand or a chair. Some people think that the postures of the body can be object of mindfulness. They think for example that the "sitting rūpa" should be object of mindfulness. Among the twenty-eight kinds of rūpa which are taught in the Abhidhamma there is no sitting rūpa. The body is composed of the four Great Elements and other rūpas which each have their own specific characteristic. The characteristic of hardness or heat may appear, no matter whether one is sitting, standing, walking or laying down. Sitting has no characteristic, it is a concept one has of the whole body which sits. In order to eradicate the idea of self who is sitting there should be awareness of one reality at a time, one nāma or rūpa. We have conditions to think of sitting and we do not have to avoid that, but we should know the difference between the moments we think of concepts such as the whole body and the moments there is awareness of a paramattha dhamma (absolute reality).

Is there any object of awareness we do not like and of which we think that it ought not to be object of awareness? Do we "push it aside" and wait until there is another object? For instance, most of us do not like it to be in a hurry. Would we rather not be aware of nāma and rūpa at such moments? Or do we think that we can't? Is there not a secret tendency not to know objects we dislike? In that way right understanding of realities cannot develop. When we are feeling tired, or angry, or when we are discouraged about the development of satipaṭṭhāna, can there be awareness even of such moments? They are only realities arising because of conditions, not self. We understand in theory that everything can be object of awareness, but do we apply this understanding? Wrong practice (sīlabbata-parāmāsā, translated as clinging to rules and ritual) is a kind of wrong view (diṭṭhi). So long as we are not sotāpanna wrong view has not been eradicated and thus wrong practice can arise. We may think that when we are in the company of many people it is impossible to be aware. Do we try to ignore particular realities we do not think fit to be objects of awareness? We can find out that although we have intellectual understanding about wrong practice such tendencies can still arise. It is essential to be aware also of these moments. If they are not known wrong view cannot be eradicated.

If one knows that whatever reality appears now can be object of awareness right understanding can develop. Should we not know seeing, hearing or thinking which appear now? When there are conditions awareness can arise in any situation, also when we are laughing or talking. We read for example in the "Khemaka Sutta" Kindred Sayings (III, Khandhā-vagga, Middle Fifty, Chapter IV, §89) that the monk Khemaka attained arahatship while he explained Dhamma to others, and that sixty monks who listened attained arahatship as well. We read in the "satipaṭṭhāna Sutta" Middle Length Sayings (I, no.10) that the Buddha, while he was staying among the Kuru people in Kammāssadhamma, spoke to the monks about the "Four Applications of Mindfulness". We read in the section on Mindfulness of the Body, on the Four Kinds of Clear Comprehension, that the Buddha said:

> '... And again, monks, a monk, when he is setting out or returning is one acting in a clearly conscious way; when he is looking in front or looking around... when he has bent in or stretched out (his arm)... when he is carrying his outer cloak, bowl and robe... when he is eating, drinking, chewing, tasting... when he is obeying the calls of nature... when he is walking, standing, sitting, asleep, awake, talking, silent, he is acting in a clearly conscious way...'

A clearly conscious way is the translation of sati-sampajañña. Is there clear comprehension with regard to the object of right understanding while we are looking in front or looking around? Is there clear comprehension while we are bending or stretching, eating, drinking, walking, standing, sitting, lying down, while we are talking or keeping silent? We may have read this text many times, but do we really apply what the Buddha taught?

42   CHAPTER 4. CLEAR COMPREHENSION

We need to consider this text often, even if we think that we have understood it already. We can find out that considering the teachings is suitable, helpful, that it is a "sappāya" for the development of understanding. This sutta can remind us that there is no limitation to the "field of awareness". When we are, for example, looking for something in our handbag, or when the shoelace breaks while tying it up, there are only nāma and rūpa, but we are likely to be forgetful. Usually dosa (aversion) arises at such moments. However, sometimes there can be awareness and then different characteristics of realities can be known. Dosa has a characteristic which is different from hardness or motion which appears through touch. Even if there is only a short moment of awareness of a reality it is helpful because it is a condition that awareness can be accumulated. In that way the tendency to take realities for self will become less.

If gocara-sampajañña is well established, there can be the fourth sampajañña, asammoha-sampajañña. Asammoha means "non-delusion". When there is asammoha-sampajañña there is non-delusion about the object of awareness. One no longer doubts whether there can be awareness while one is busy or while one is in trying circumstances. When there is no delusion the realities appearing through the six doors can be known as they are, as not self. When there is awareness of visible object there is no delusion about visible object, it is realized as just a reality, not a person or a thing.

It is useful to know the different aspects of clear comprehension, sati-sampajañña: clear comprehension with regard to the purpose, with regard to what is suitable, with regard to the object of sati and clear comprehension of non-delusion. However, while right understanding is being developed we do not have to try to pinpoint which kind of sampajañña arises. It is sati-sampajañña, not self, which knows the purpose of the development of the Eightfold Path, the eradication of defilements. It is sati-sampajañña which knows the right conditions which are suitable for the development of right understanding. In the beginning one still doubts whether there can be awareness in any situation, one limits the field of sati, and thus there cannot yet be non-delusion about the object of awareness.

You think that there are particular factors which can hinder awareness, such as our working situation or the company of other people. The place where we are, the people we meet, noise, travelling, sickness, all these factors are not impediments for satipaṭṭhāna. Wrong understanding of the path is a hindrance.

In the Visuddhimagga (III, 29) we read about the ten impediments. These are: dwelling, family, gain, class (students), building, travel, relatives, affliction (sickness), books and supernormal powers. As regards dwelling, for those who cultivate samatha the dwelling is only an impediment if it distracts one or if one has many belongings stored there. As regards family, this refers to relatives or a family of supporters who present food or other requisites to the monk. They can be distracting from the development of calm. As regards gain, this means here the four requisites of the monk. If he receives requisites from people all the time, he has to give them blessings and teach them Dhamma. In this way he will be engaged continuously. Class means students of suttas or students of Abhidhamma. If the monk has to teach students he has no opportunity for the development of samatha. Building means the construction of a building. This is always an impediment for samatha since one is engaged in seeing to the work. Travel is an impediment for samatha since one's thoughts are occupied with the journey. With the impediment of relatives is also meant the monk's teacher or pupil or others he is dwelling together with. If they are sick they are an impediment for samatha since they preoccupy him. Affliction is any kind of illness. It is an impediment when it causes suffering. As regards books, this is responsibility for the scriptures, or recitation of the scriptures. When he is engaged with these matters it will distract him from the development of samatha.

44 CHAPTER 4. CLEAR COMPREHENSION

It is said that nine of the ten impediments are hindrances only for samatha. They distract one from its cultivation. As regards the tenth impediment, which are the supernatural powers of the non-ariyan, this is not a hindrance for samatha. We read in the Visuddhimagga (III, 56) about the super-normal powers:

> 'They are hard to maintain, like a prone infant or like a baby hare, and the slightest thing breaks them. But they are an impediment for insight, not for concentration, since they are obtainable through concentration. So the supernormal powers are an impediment that should be severed by one who seeks insight; the others are impediments to be severed by one who seeks concentration.'

By these examples one sees that the method and aim of samatha is different from the method and aim of vipassanā. If one has accumulations to develop calm to a high degree one has to live a secluded life and the factors which are impediments to calm have to be severed. As regards insight, this has to be developed in one's daily life, one has to develop understanding of all realities which appear, one's defilements included. As we have seen, only super-normal powers are an impediment for insight since one cannot lead one's daily life if one wants to develop them. One has to live in seclusion and one has to develop calm to the degree of jhāna in order to be able to acquire the supernormal powers. The other factors which are impediments for samatha are not impediments for vipassanā. "Dwelling" is not a hindrance for the development of insight. We still have attachment to our house, we want to embellish it. So long as one is not an anāgāmī (non-returner), attachment to sensuous objects has not been eradicated yet. Attachment to the place where we live and any other kind of attachment can be object of awareness when it appears and then it is not an impediment. If there is no right understanding of the object of satipaṭṭhāna., everything hinders: the place where one lives, relatives, travelling or sickness. There always seems to be an excuse for not being aware right at this moment. First this work has to be finished, that letter has to be written, relatives need help and take up our time so that we believe that there is no opportunity for awareness. What is hindering us now? Are there not nāma and rūpa, right at this moment? There is impingement of hardness or softness on the body-sense, wherever we are. Hardness is a paramattha dhamma, an absolute reality, but when there is no awareness we do not know it as a reality. We may be thinking of hardness but that is not awareness. When sati-sampajañña arises the characteristic of hardness can be studied without there being the need to think about it. It can be known as a reality which is conditioned. It does not belong to anyone; we cannot change it, we cannot do anything about it.

One may think that awareness is too difficult, one may believe that one should first go to a quiet place. Why is that? Because one expects many moments of awareness and immediate clear comprehension. We should let go of expectations. If we have listened to the Dhamma and if we have understood the way to develop right understanding of nāma and rūpa, there are conditions for the arising of awareness. After a moment of awareness there are bound to be countless moments of unawareness since we accumulated ignorance for aeons. How could we get rid of it within a short time? If we think that awareness in daily life is too difficult we create a hindrance for the development of right understanding. If there is a beginning of the development of understanding now it can be accumulated. If that would be impossible there would be no ariyans who have realized the truth. They have proved that there are no impediments to the development of right understanding in daily life.

With mettā,

Nina van Gorkom

5

Nāma and rūpa

Tokyo
April 10
1971

Dear Mr. G.,

You asked me about the way to know the difference between nāma and rūpa. You find it difficult to realize their different characteristics. I will first summarize the points that you have doubts about:

When feeling hot, there are both nāma and rūpa. What is the characteristic of body-consciousness (kaya-viññāṇa)? What is the characteristic of bodily feeling which accompanies body-consciousness? What are the characteristics of other feelings besides bodily feeling which arise at other moments? What is the characteristic of the rūpa which is heat?

These are questions which are bound to arise when we learn about different nāmas and rūpas and we begin to be aware of them. There are different levels of understanding of realities. First there should be theoretical understanding about nāma and rūpa, and then one can begin to be aware of their characteristics when they appear. Through awareness direct understanding of realities can be developed.

Body-consciousness is the citta which experiences rūpas which impinge on the body-sense. These rūpas can be the following: the "Element of Earth" or solidity, to be experienced as hardness or softness; the "Element of Fire", to be experienced as heat or cold; the "Element of Wind", to be experienced as motion or pressure. These rūpas impinge on the body-sense all the time. The body-sense through which these rūpas can be experienced is also rūpa. The body-sense does not know anything, but it is a condition for the nāma which experiences tangible object. The body-sense is to be found all over the body, except in those parts which are insensitive, such as hair or nails. The body-sense is not only on the outside of the body, but also inside the body. The Visuddhimagga (XIV, 52) states that it is to be found everywhere, like a liquid that soaks a layer of cotton. Also in those parts of the body we call "kidney" or "liver" there is body-sense; pain can be felt in these parts. When we notice any bodily sensation, be it ever so slight, it shows that there is impact on the body-sense. When we remember this it can be a condition for awareness of different kinds of realities, also when the impact on the body-sense is very slight, or inside the body.

All day long rūpas impinge on the body-sense but we do not realize that they are only rūpas. We always think of a being, the body or a thing which is touched, but these do not impinge on the body-sense. The experience of tangible object through the body-sense is one moment, and the thinking of stories about that object is another moment. There are different realities appearing at different moments through different doorways. This is the truth and it can be proven by our own experience. Body-consciousness which experiences tangible object impinging on the body-sense is vipāka-citta, a citta which is the result of kamma. When it experiences a pleasant tangible object it is the result of kusala kamma and when it experiences an unpleasant object it is the result of akusala kamma. When the object which impinges on the body-sense is pleasant the body-consciousness is accompanied by pleasant (bodily) feeling, and when the object is unpleasant the body-consciousness is accompanied by painful (bodily) feeling. There cannot be indifferent bodily feeling. The object is unpleasant when the temperature which impinges on the body-sense is too cold or too hot, and it is pleasant when the temperature is just right.

The pleasant feeling or painful feeling which accompanies body-consciousness is nāma, it experiences something. It is different from rūpa which does not experience anything. Since body-consciousness is vipāka, the accompanying feeling is also vipāka.

Body-consciousness which experiences tangible object arises in a process of cittas which experience that object. Each citta in a process performs it own function while it experiences the object which is impinging. The body-consciousness which is vipāka-citta falls away immediately and it is succeeded by other cittas. There are cittas arising within the process which can be kusala citta or akusala citta and they experience the same object as the body-consciousness. When they are kusala cittas they can be accompanied by happy (mental) feeling or by indifferent feeling, and when they are akusala cittas, they can be accompanied by happy (mental) feeling, by indifferent feeling or by unhappy (mental) feeling. These feelings can be called "mental feeling" in order to differentiate them from the bodily feeling which accompanies body-consciousness. As we have seen, bodily feeling is not rūpa, it is nāma. It can be called bodily feeling since it accompanies body-consciousness.

Sometimes we have an idea that painful feeling and aversion which can arise shortly afterwards can hardly be separated. However, they are different realities arising because of different conditions. When we burn ourselves the heat, which is an unpleasant tangible object, impinges on the body-sense and it is experienced by body-consciousness which is accompanied by painful bodily feeling. At that moment there is no dislike, the body-consciousness which is vipāka-citta, the result of kamma, merely experiences the unpleasant object. The painful feeling which accompanies the body-consciousness is also vipāka. It merely feels, it does not dislike the object. The citta with aversion, the dosa-mūla-citta, which is accompanied by mental unpleasant feeling arises later on. It experiences the object with aversion, it is akusala citta. When sati arises it can be mindful of one reality at a time, and thus gradually different characteristics of realities can be known. If we try to "catch" realities and if we have desire to know whether the reality which appears is citta, feeling, rūpa or any other phenomenon, there is thinking with attachment, not mindfulness.

You wrote that you find that attachment, lobha, and aversion, dosa, can be known more easily than seeing or hearing. Can we say that anything is easy? We may think that it is easy to know lobha and dosa but do we realize their characteristics when they appear? Or are we merely thinking about them? Do we know them as conditioned nāmas, not self or is there still "my lobha" and "my dosa"? We should realize lobha and dosa also when they are of a lesser degree. For example, when there is seeing there is bound to be clinging to what is seen or clinging to seeing, arising closely after the seeing. When we hear a sound which is loud there can be a slight aversion but we may not even notice it. When there is lobha or dosa there are nāma and rūpa, there are so many realities we are still ignorant of. Lobha and dosa condition rūpas. Don't we look different when we are angry or when we are glad? When we are afraid or when we dislike something we may notice bodily phenomena conditioned by citta. It is not easy to distinguish between the different characteristics of realities. We tend to join different realities into a "whole" of "my personality" and thus we will not know them as they are, only nāma and rūpa, devoid of self.

In your letter you gave examples of moments of awareness. You write that when walking you are aware of the feeling of pressing the ground. Is there not thinking of a concept of "pressing the ground"? Do you picture yourself as walking? That is a way of thinking. The object one thinks of at that moment is a concept or idea, not a reality. We may easily mislead ourselves and take thinking for awareness. When you touch hardness and you know that it is hard is there clear understanding of the true nature of the rūpa which is hardness? There may still be "something" hard there which seems to stay. Does the ground seem to stay? Even when one does not name it "ground" or "feet" there can still be wrong understanding of reality. The rūpa which is hardness can be experienced through the body-sense and it arises and falls away, it cannot stay. Hardness seems to stay so long as we have not understood the truth of impermanence. We cling to sati and we want to hold on to realities in order to know them. We should not expect there to be full understanding of nāma and rūpa which arise and fall away, but we can learn to be aware of one characteristic of reality at a time when it appears. When we remember that realities and also awareness cannot last we will be less inclined to try to be aware and to hold on to realities. When it is the right time for sati it arises and then it can be aware of any reality which appears. We cannot plan to be aware of such or such reality.

You write that when eating you are aware of flavour. There is not only flavour, there is also the nāma which experiences flavour, otherwise flavour could not appear. Do we know already the difference between nāma and rūpa? There can be mindfulness of only one reality at a time, but it seems that flavour and the experience of it appear together. When understanding develops one reality can be known at a time, but now there is still confusion. You say that you can be aware of the movement of the jaws when eating. Again, is there not thinking of the idea of "my jaws" instead of being aware of one nāma or rūpa at a time? When we become more familiar with the characteristics of nāma and rūpa we will be less inclined to name them or to select a particular object of awareness.

Some people may be inclined to sit and wait for the appearing of hearing, sound, like or dislike. In that way realities will not be known. We can go on with all the things we usually do and we do not have to do anything special in order to have awareness. For instance, when one is writing, there may be sound, hearing, like, dislike or any other reality. When moving the hand hardness or motion may appear and these realities can be object of awareness. We should not mind what kind of reality presents itself. One may be trying to "catch" the difference between hearing and sound, seeing and visible object, but in that way realities will not be known. Sometimes there may be mindfulness of rūpa, sometimes of nāma, it all depends on the sati. I am glad to hear that while you talk there can also be awareness. One may be inclined to think that it is impossible to be aware while talking, since one has to think of what one is going to say. Now you can prove to yourself that also at such moments there are nāmas and rūpas appearing. The thinking which occurs while one is talking is also a reality which can be object of awareness. If there never is awareness of thinking one cannot learn that thinking is anattā.

Our life consists of nāma and rūpa. When there is the development of awareness everything appears as usual, but before we did not know that what appears is a characteristic of reality. There is hearing, seeing or feeling all the time, but when there is no awareness we do not realize that they are only conditioned realities, nāmas. There is a reality at every moment but when we are forgetful we do not realize this. We should develop right understanding until we are familiar with the characteristics which appear, until there is no more doubt about them. When we are hungry or when we have a headache there are different kinds of nāma and rūpa. There is rūpa such as hardness, there are nāmas such as painful bodily feeling or unhappy mental feeling, there are many realities appearing. If there is no awareness when there is painful feeling we will think that pain can last for a while. When there is mindfulness we can find out that there are many other kinds of nāma and rūpa presenting themselves besides the pain caused by the impact on the body-sense. Pain does not stay, it falls away immediately, and then it arises again.

We find our likes and dislikes very important. We let ourselves be carried away by like and dislike instead of being aware of different realities. We read in the Kindred Sayings (IV, Saḷāyatana-vagga, Kindred Sayings on Sense, Third Fifty, Chapter III, §130, Hāliddaka):

> Once the venerable Kaccāna the Great was staying among the folk of Avanti, at Osprey's Haunt, on a sheer mountain crag. Then the housefather Hāliddakāni came to the venerable Kaccāna the Great. Seated at one side he said this:- 'It has been said by the Exalted One, sir, "Owing to diversity in elements arises diversity of contact. Owing to diversity of contact arises diversity of feeling". Pray, sir, how far is this so?'
> 'Herein, housefather, after having seen a pleasant object with the eye, a monk comes to know as such eye-consciousness that is a pleasant experience. Owing to contact that is pleasant to experience arises happy feeling.

After having seen with the eye an object that is unpleasant, a monk comes to know as such eye-consciousness that is an unpleasant experience. Owing to contact that is unpleasant to experience arises unhappy feeling.

After having seen with the eye an object that is of indifferent effect, a monk comes to know as such eye-consciousness that experiences an object which is of indifferent effect. Owing to contact that is indifferent to experience arises feeling that is indifferent.

So also, housefather, after having heard a sound with the ear, smelt a scent with the nose, tasted a flavour with the tongue, experienced tangible object with the body, cognized with the mind a mental object, that is pleasant... Owing to contact that is pleasant to experience arises happy feeling. But after having cognized a mental object which is unpleasant... owing to contact that is unpleasant to experience arises unhappy feeling. Again, after having cognized with the mind a mental object that is indifferent in effect, he comes to know as such mind-consciousness that experiences an object which is of indifferent effect. Owing to contact that is indifferent arises feeling that is indifferent.

Thus, housefather, owing to diversity in elements arises diversity of contact. Owing to diversity of contact arises diversity of feeling.'

We do not come to know seeing, visible object, contact and feeling "as such" merely by just thinking about them. Paññā should realize the characteristic of seeing when it presents itself; it should realize seeing as nāma which arises because of conditions, not self. The nāma which sees is different from the rūpa which is visible object. When we learn to see realities as elements which arise because of conditions and which we cannot control, we will be less carried away by pleasant or unpleasant objects. We are attached to the feelings which arise on account of the objects which are experienced. Feeling accompanies each citta but we are mostly forgetful of feeling. Is there any understanding of the feeling which presents itself now? If there never is awareness of feeling there cannot be detachment from the idea of "my feeling".

There are realities appearing through the six doors, wherever we are. There is no need to go to a quiet place in order to know them. When we are in the company of many people, for example at a party, there are only realities appearing through the six doors and gradually we can learn to be aware of them. We see pleasant objects and on account of these we feel happy. However, we can remember that it is only feeling which feels, feeling which has arisen because of pleasant contact. We will see or hear unpleasant objects and owing to the unpleasant contact unhappy feeling is bound to arise. We will get tired when we have to stand for a long time while we listen to speeches and we may feel tense. There are only different realities appearing such as hardness or aversion. All the time there is diversity of elements, diversity of contact and owing to that contact diversity of feeling. We can consider the Dhamma wherever we are and if there is no clinging to sati there can be conditions for its arising. There cannot yet be the precise knowledge of realities but we can begin to learn.

With mettā,

Nina van Gorkom

6
Direct experience

Tokyo
April 20
1971

Dear Mr. G.,

I will repeat your question: There is awareness, but not often of characteristics of nāma and rūpa. How can I get to know directly characteristics of realities?

Is there seeing now? It has a characteristic which can be directly experienced. It is a reality which can experience visible object through the eye-door. It is a type of nāma, not self.

Is there hearing now? That is another reality. It is a type of nāma which experiences sound through the ear-door. Hardness, softness, heat or cold appear time and again. They are different realities which each have their own characteristic. A characteristic of nāma or rūpa is not something besides that which can be experienced now, at this moment. All realities which appear have different characteristics and they can be experienced one at a time. Seeing is nāma, visible object is rūpa; they have different characteristics.

You wrote that you cannot distinguish the difference between seeing and thinking about what was seen, that they seem to occur at the same time. When we pay attention to the shape and form of something such as a chair there is thinking. However, are there not also moments of merely experiencing what appears through the eye-sense, without there being thinking? There is not all the time thinking or defining of what something is. There are moments of seeing and seeing conditions thinking about what was seen, but they occur at different moments. One citta can have only one object at a time. We cannot expect to have precise understanding of realities, but we can begin to be aware of different realities. There are different degrees of knowing characteristics of nāma and rūpa and when paññā has been developed more, they will be known more clearly. They have to be known as nāma and as rūpa, not self.

The Buddha explained realities in different ways so that people would be able to know them as nāma elements and rūpa elements, as not self. We read in "An Exhortation from Nandaka" Middle Length Sayings (III, no.146) that the monk Nandaka had to preach to the nuns. Then the Buddha asked him to repeat to them exactly the same sermon. Why? Their "faculties", indriyas, were developed and hearing the same sermon again would be the right condition for them to attain the degree of enlightenment for which they were ripe. How could that happen? Could it be just because they were listening and thinking about what they heard, or rather because there would be mindfulness while listening? While listening mindfulness can arise and it can be aware of seeing, hearing, thinking or feeling, of any reality appearing through one of the six doors. When I quote what Nandaka said, one may think, "Is that all?" However, when one listens, considers what one has heard and there can be mindfulness of realities one can come to know them as they are.

The conversation between Nandaka and the nuns reads:

> "What do you think about this, sisters? Is the eye permanent or impermanent?"
> "Impermanent, revered sir."
> "But is what is impermanent anguish or happiness?"
> "Anguish, revered sir."
> "Is it right to regard that which is impermanent, anguish and liable to alteration as, 'This is mine, this am I, this is myself'?"
> "No, revered sir."
> "What do you think about this, sisters? Is the ear... the nose... the tongue... the body-sense... the mind, permanent or impermanent? Is it right to regard that which is impermanent, anguish and liable to alteration as, 'This is mine, this am I, this is myself?' "
> "No, revered sir. What is the reason for this? Already, revered sir, by means of perfect intuitive wisdom it has been well seen by us as it really is that, 'These six internal sense-fields are impermanent' ".

The six "internal sense-fields" (āyatanas) are the five senses and the mind. The same is said about the six "external sense-fields": colours, sounds, smells, flavours, tangibles and mental objects. The same is said about the "six classes of consciousness" which experience these objects. Then Nandaka said:

"It is good, sisters, it is good. For it is thus, sisters, that by means of perfect intuitive wisdom this is seen by an ariyan disciple as it really is. It is, sisters, like the oil for lighting an oil-lamp which is impermanent and liable to alteration, and like the wick which is impermanent and liable to alteration, and like the flame which is impermanent and liable to alteration, and like the light which is impermanent and liable to alteration. If anyone, sisters, were to speak thus: 'The oil for lighting this oil-lamp is impermanent and liable to alteration, and the wick... and the flame is impermanent and liable to alteration, but that which is the light–that is permanent, lasting, eternal, not liable to alteration', speaking thus, sisters, would he be speaking rightly?"

"No, revered sir. What is the reason for this? It is, revered sir, that if the oil for lighting this oil-lamp be impermanent and liable to alteration, and if the wick... and if the flame be impermanent and liable to alteration, all the more is the light impermanent and liable to alteration."

"Even so, sisters, if anyone should speak thus: 'These six internal sense-fields are impermanent and liable to alteration, but whatever pleasure or pain or indifferent feeling I experience as a result of these six internal sense-fields, that is permanent, lasting, eternal, not liable to alteration.' speaking thus, sisters, would he be speaking rightly?" "No, revered sir. What is the reason for this? As a result of this or that condition, revered sir, these or those feelings arise. From the stopping of this or that condition these or those feelings are stopped."

You wrote that awareness helps you to be less involved when

unpleasant things happen. Sometimes there are conditions for sati and paññā, but when feelings are intense we tend to take them for self, we find it very difficult to see them as only conditioned realities, only nāma. Usually we are absorbed in what appears through eyes, ears, nose, tongue, body-sense and mind, and we are forgetful of realities.

At times we have to experience unpleasant objects through the senses. The other day someone hit me, meaning it as a joke. Feeling the impact of it was akusala vipāka through the body-sense. Why did this have to happen to me? At such moments one may be upset and there is no awareness. Of course, I know why it happened: it was the result of akusala kamma, a deed committed in the past. Thus we see that everything we have to experience are only conditioned realities, and also our like or dislike of what happens and our feelings about it are only conditioned realities. Our attachment or our dislike are not vipāka, they arise with akusala citta which is conditioned by our accumulated defilements. We had attachment and aversion in the past and therefore there are conditions for their arising today. There are different types of conditions which play their part in our life.

Now I shall continue with the sutta. Further on we read that Nandaka said:

> "It is good, sisters, it is good. For it is thus, sisters, that by means of perfect intuitive wisdom this is seen by an ariyan disciple as it really is. It is, sisters, as if a clever cattle-butcher or a cattle-butcher's apprentice, having killed a cow, should dissect the cow with a butcher's sharp knife without spoiling the flesh within, without spoiling the outer hide, and with the butcher's sharp knife should cut, should cut around, should cut all around whatever tendons, sinews and ligaments there are within; and

having cut, cut around, cut all around and removed the outer hide and, having clothed that cow in that self-same hide again, should then speak thus: 'This cow is conjoined with this hide as before.' Speaking thus, sisters, would he be speaking rightly?"

"No, revered sir. What is the reason for this? Although, revered sir, that clever cattle-butcher or cattle-butcher's apprentice, having killed a cow... having clothed that cow in that self-same hide again, might then speak thus: 'This cow is conjoined with this hide as before,' yet that cow is not conjoined with that hide."

"I have made this simile for you, sisters, so as to illustrate the meaning. This is the meaning here: 'the flesh within' sisters, is a synonym for the six internal sense-fields.'The outer hide', sisters, is a synonym for the six external sense-fields.'The tendons, sinews and ligaments within', sisters, is a synonym for delight and attachment. 'The butcher's sharp knife', sisters, is a synonym for the ariyan intuitive wisdom, the ariyan intuitive wisdom by which one cuts, cuts around, cuts all around the inner defilements, the inner fetters and the inner bonds."

After Nandaka had finished his sermon and the nuns had departed, the Buddha said to the monks: "...although these nuns were delighted with Nandaka's teaching on Dhamma, their aspirations were not fulfilled."

We then read:

Then the Lord addressed the venerable Nandaka, saying:
"Well then, Nandaka, you may exhort these nuns with this same exhortation again tomorrow."

We read that after Nandaka had given the same sermon to the nuns for the second time the Buddha said:

"...these nuns were delighted with Nandaka's teaching on Dhamma and their aspirations were fulfilled. She who is the last nun of these five hundred nuns is a stream-winner (sotāpanna), not liable to the Downfall; she is assured, bound for self-awakening."

You might think that the nuns had understood the impermanence of conditioned realities already the first time, but there are many degrees of realizing the truth. The hearing of Nandaka's sermon for the second time was a condition for those who had not attained enlightenment to become sotāpanna, and for others who were already ariyans to attain higher stages of enlightenment. Thus we can see that listening to the teachings or reading the scriptures are conditions for mindfulness and the development of paññā, and even for attaining enlightenment.

This sutta illustrates that the Buddha taught about all realities which can be experienced through the six doors. They appear all the time in daily life. Right understanding should be developed of these realities, there is no other way. Some people think that one should select particular objects of awareness, they believe that one should not be aware of all objects which appear. This is not the development of the Eightfold Path. If one is, for example, never aware of visible object which appears through the eyes one will continue to believe that people can be experienced through the eye-sense. In reality only the rūpa which is visible object can be seen, but one is unable to eliminate the idea of "being" from the visible object. One should check whether paññā can eliminate doubt and ignorance about the characteristics of nāma and rūpa or not yet. It is not sufficient to be aware of what appears through one door only. When the nuns listened to Nandaka's sermon they were considering and studying with awareness the characteristics of nāma and rūpa which appeared in order to understand them thoroughly. One should not merely repeat for oneself what one has heard about nāma and rūpa or merely follow what one's teacher said. One should develop understanding oneself of whatever appears through one of the six doors. One may believe that seeing and hearing are very clear, but this may be only thinking, not direct understanding of these realities. There should be the development of right understanding which knows nāma as nāma and rūpa as rūpa. Usually one is so absorbed in the object which appears that one forgets to be aware of the nāma which experiences the object. When visible object appears it is evident that there is also a reality which experiences it, a type of nāma. If there were no nāma which experiences visible object how could visible object appear? It is seeing which sees, no self who sees. There can be awareness of one reality at a time, a nāma or a rūpa and then one can learn their different characteristics.

In the above quoted sutta we read about the dissecting of a cow. When it has been dissected there is no longer the idea of a whole cow. When we join realities together into a "whole" there is the idea of a thing, a person, a self. When paññā directly realizes visible object as rūpa, not self, hardness as rūpa, not self, hearing as nāma, not self, and the other realities appearing one at a time as not self, the concept of a whole will disappear.

After I had typed the text about dissecting the cow, my husband and I were having dinner. While we were eating I was still busy "dissecting the cow". I liked the food and I remembered the words of the sutta that we are bound by delight and attachment. We are bound by these "tendons", but wisdom can cut them away. The scriptures can be a condition to consider different nāmas and rūpas which appear in daily life. We are bound by attachment and delight with regard to what is experienced through the six doors. We like savours and tasting, we want to go on tasting. We like visible object and seeing, we want to go on seeing. We like sound and hearing, we want to go on hearing.

We like thoughts and thinking, we want to go on thinking. Thus there are conditions to go on in the cycle of birth and death. It is because of clinging that we must be reborn. There will be the arising of nāma and rūpa in other existences, again and again.

Why did the nuns have to hear the same sermon again? Hearing it only once was not enough. We also would need to hear it again and again, many more times. We still cling to the internal sense-fields and the external sense-fields. That is why it is necessary to be aware of seeing, visible object, hearing, sound, of all realities which appear through the six doors, over and over again, without preference for a particular reality, without excluding any reality. Thus we have to be busy, "dissecting the cow ". You asked me how we can realize the conditions for nāma and rūpa through being aware of them, and whether that is different from thinking about conditions.

There are different degrees of understanding conditions. We can have theoretical understanding of the fact that eye-sense is a condition for seeing. Without eye-sense there cannot be seeing. Seeing sees visible object or colour. Visible object is a condition for seeing by being its object. Seeing is vipāka-citta, it is produced by kamma. Kamma-condition is another type of condition. There are different types of conditions for the realities which arise.

Theoretical understanding of conditions is not the same as paññā which directly knows conditions for the nāma and rūpa which appear. This is a stage of insight which cannot arise before the beginning stage of insight which is the stage that paññā clearly distinguishes the difference between the characteristic of nāma and the characteristic of rūpa. Seeing is a reality which experiences visible object, it is not self but nāma. There is no need to think about this. Can the characteristic of seeing not be known when it appears? Seeing is different from visible object. Visible object is rūpa, it does not know anything. Hearing is a reality which experiences sound. It is different from sound which is rūpa, a reality which does not know anything. Through awareness of nāma and rūpa which appear one at a time paññā can come to realize that nāma is different from rūpa. When the first stage of insight arises there is no idea of a "whole", there are only different elements appearing one at a time. There is no idea of self who realizes nāma as nāma and rūpa as rūpa, but it is paññā which realizes this. How could paññā directly know conditions for nāma and rūpa when the difference between these realities has not been discerned yet? This would be impossible. Do seeing and visible object not seem to appear at the same time? Do hearing and sound not seem to appear at the same time? Do seeing and hearing not seem to appear at the same time? Is there an idea of the whole body? Don't we join all realities together into a "whole"? Is there not the whole of the world, the whole of a being, the whole of our personality? Is there an idea of self who is aware? We still have to study, to be aware of different realities, to discern their different characteristics. We have to learn such a great deal before the first stage of insight can arise. We don't even know whether it can arise during this life, that depends on understanding which has been accumulated, also in past lives. It is after the first stage of insight that paññā can come to know directly nāma and rūpa as conditioned realities. This does not mean that there has to be thinking about all the different conditions for each reality. This stage of insight is different from our intellectual understanding at this moment of the different conditions for nāma and rūpa.

Some people think that knowing the conditions for aversion, dosa, would help to eliminate it. They think that knowing the conditions means thinking about the circumstances, the "story". However, that is not paññā which realizes conditions, it is thinking of concepts. Is there not an idea of "my dosa" about which one thinks? The way to eliminate dosa is the development of right understanding of all realities which appear. Only when one has attained the third stage of enlightenment dosa can be eradicated. It cannot be eradicated so long as the wrong view of self has not been eradicated. When dosa appears its characteristic can be studied so that it can be realized as only a conditioned reality, not "my dosa". The real cause of dosa is not the circumstances, not the other people. Our accumulations of dosa condition its arising. There were countless moments of dosa in the past and thus it can arise today. There is ignorance accompanying each moment of dosa, thus ignorance is a condition for it. There is no attachment, lobha, at the same time as dosa, but lobha is also a condition for dosa. We like pleasant objects and when the object is unpleasant there is aversion, we dislike it when we don't get what we want. Thus we see that there are several conditioning factors for realities, some of which arise at the same time and some of which do not arise at the same time. When we think about the "story", about the circumstances of dosa we do not come to know more about the reality of dosa. We have accumulations to think a great deal. When there is thinking it can be realized as just nāma, not self.

Ignorance about realities can never be eradicated by thinking. The Buddha explained about the realities appearing through the six doors in order to remind us to be aware of them over and over again. Only in that way ignorance and wrong view of realities can be eradicated.

We read in the Kindred Sayings (IV, Saḷāyatana-vagga, Second Fifty, Chapter I, §53, Ignorance):

> Then a certain monk came to the Exalted One, and on coming to him saluted him and sat down at one side. So seated that monk said this:
> "By how knowing, lord, by how seeing does ignorance vanish and knowledge arise?"
> "In him who knows and sees the eye as impermanent, monk, ignorance vanishes and knowledge arises. In him who knows and sees visible objects... seeing-

consciousness...the ear...sounds...hearing-consciousness...the tongue...flavours...tasting-consciousness...the nose...smells... consciousness...the body...touches...body-consciousness...the mind...mind-states...mind-consciousness...as impermanent, ignorance vanishes and knowledge arises."

With mettā,

Nina van Gorkom

7
Concentration on Breathing

Tokyo
May 10
1971

Dear Mr. G.,

You wrote to me about concentration on breathing and since many people are interested in this subject I will quote from your letter:

I find that while I concentrate on breathing sensations and thoughts are blotted out and in this way I become more relaxed and I have less aversion. I find that after this exercise mindfulness becomes more acute and frequent. Seeing and hearing seem so clear, and all six doors are wide open, registering with clarity and intensity everything. The situation is like a spider in a web, ready to catch, but without tension. I find that by means of concentration on breathing, I can create favourable conditions for wisdom of the Eightfold Path. I believe that I can be mindful more often when I am relaxed.

Your letter raises many questions with regard to samatha and vipassanā. Some people have accumulations to develop both samatha and vipassanā; others develop only samatha and others again only vipassanā. Both for the development of samatha and for the development of vipassanā, it is essential to have right understanding of the way of development. It is felt by some that for samatha it is not necessary to know about realities, to know one's different types of citta, since one should, as they believe, just concentrate until sense-impressions are "blotted out". However, this is not the right way of development. If one starts to concentrate for example on breathing, without understanding when the citta is kusala citta and when akusala citta, one will take attachment to breathing for the calm which accompanies kusala citta. One does not know the difference between samatha and what is not samatha but merely a breathing-exercise. When one has a sensation of sense-impressions being blotted out one mistakenly believes that one has attained jhāna (absorption). We should understand which cause brings which effect. If one wants to apply oneself to mindfulness of breathing one should note that just concentration on one's breathing is not samatha. People concentrate on their breathing for various reasons: for example because it is good for one's health and it makes one feel more relaxed.

Mindfulness of breathing is among the meditation subjects of samatha and as such it is quite different from any other kind of concentration on breathing. The aim of samatha is to be less attached to sense-impressions, and, in order to reach this aim, it is essential that there is right understanding of the way to develop true calm. True calm is wholesome, at that moment there are

71

no lobha, dosa or moha. We read about people in the Buddha's time who could develop calm to the degree of jhāna. When jhāna is attained defilements are temporarily eliminated, but they are not eradicated. There are many misunderstandings about the development of samatha and if it is not developed in the right way one develops wrong concentration, micchā-samādhi, instead of calm.

I have heard people say that they want to become less restless and to have more calm, and that they therefore want to apply themselves to samatha. However, do they know the real meaning of restlessness and calm? "Restlessness", in Pāli uddhacca, is akusala. It is a cetasika which arises with each akusala citta: with lobha-mūla-citta (citta rooted in attachment), with dosa-mūla-citta (citta rooted in aversion) and with moha-mūla-citta (citta rooted in ignorance). It prevents the citta from wholesomeness. Uddhacca is different from what one in conventional language calls "restlessness". When we use the word "restlessness" in conventional language we usually think of aversion and unpleasant feeling. People dislike unpleasant feeling and they like pleasant feeling or indifferent feeling. However, pleasant feeling and indifferent feeling can accompany both kusala citta and akusala citta. If one pays attention only to feeling and one does not know when the citta is kusala citta and when akusala citta one's life is very confused. For instance, when one is in quiet surroundings, one may be attached to quietness and thus there are at that moment lobha-mūla-cittas which can be accompanied by pleasant feeling or by indifferent feeling. Since lobha-mūla-citta is akusala citta it is accompanied by restlessness. Or, there may be moha-mūla-cittas which are accompanied by indifferent feeling. Moha-mūla-citta is also accompanied by restlessness. Thus, when the feeling is pleasant or indifferent, the citta may be akusala citta and in that case it is inevitably accompanied by restlessness. Although one believes that one is calm at that moment, one still has restlessness. Do we realize it whether the pleasant feeling or indifferent feeling which arises is kusala or akusala? We have theoretical knowledge of kusala and akusala, but in order to develop what is wholesome we must know whether the citta at this moment is kusala or akusala. Attachment to calm may be very subtle, one may not notice it. Lobha can lure us all the time. Only paññā can know whether the citta which arises is kusala or akusala.

In conventional language we use the word "calm". We should know which kind of reality calm is. Calm, in Pāli passaddhi, is a cetasika. In fact, there are two cetasikas: kāya-passaddhi, tranquillity of body, and citta-passaddhi, tranquillity of mind. By kāya, body, is meant here the "mental body", which are the cetasikas (the three nāma-kkhandhas which are vedāna-kkhandha, feeling, saññā-kkhandha, perception, and saṅkhāra-kkhandha, the "formations") as distinct from citta (Visuddhimagga XIV, 144). Thus, there is calm of cetasikas and calm of citta. We read in the Visuddhimagga (XIV, 144):

> '...But both tranquillity of that body and of consciousness have, together, the characteristic of quieting disturbance of that body and of consciousness. Their function is to crush disturbance of the (mental) body and of consciousness. They are manifested as inactivity and coolness of the (mental) body and of consciousness...'

The two cetasikas which are calm of "body" and calm of citta arise with each kusala citta, no matter whether one is performing dāna (generosity), observing sīla (morality), developing samatha or vipassanā. Thus, also while we are generous or abstain from lying there is calm: at such moments there are no lobha, dosa or moha accompanying the citta. When there are moments of mettā, lovingkindness, towards someone we meet, there is true calm. Mettā is a subject of samatha, but it can and should be developed in daily life, when we are in the company of other people. We should not confuse mettā with selfish affection, we should know that when there is pure lovingkindness we do not expect anything in return, we do not want anything for ourselves. When we hear the word samatha we may think that one has to develop it in quiet surroundings until jhāna is attained. However, there can be moments of calm, samatha, in daily life if there is right understanding, paññā, which knows when the citta is kusala citta and when akusala citta. We should not believe that this is easy. Those who have accumulations for jhāna can develop calm to the degree of jhāna, but only very few people are able to. We do not know whether there are at the present time people who are able to attain jhāna. When jhāna is attained defilements are temporarily eliminated.

There is calm when one develops vipassanā. When one is aware of a characteristic of nāma or rūpa there is kusala citta which is accompanied by calm. Moreover, vipassanā leads to the eradication of wrong view and the other defilements. The arahat has eradicated all latent tendencies of defilements and thus he has the highest degree of calm.

When the citta is not intent on dāna, sīla or bhāvanā, mental development, there is no calm, passaddhi. Concentration on breathing with the aim to become relaxed is not a way of kusala kamma, it is not samatha. There is then no passaddhi with the citta, even if one thinks that one is feeling calm. At such a moment there may not be dosa, but lobha and moha are bound to arise.

Right understanding of what is kusala and what is akusala will prevent us from taking for samatha what is not samatha. If one believes that one can develop calm to the degree of jhāna, one should know about the many conditions which have to be fulfilled in order to attain it. If one understands how difficult it is to attain jhāna one will not mislead oneself and believe that one has attained it when there is a sensation of sense-impressions being blotted out or other unusual experiences. The person who wants to develop samatha to the degree of jhāna should lead a secluded life and he should not spend his time with various entertainments such as one enjoys while leading a worldly life. One should really see the disadvantages of sense-pleasures and one should have the intention to cultivate the conditions for being away from them. If the right conditions are not fulfilled there cannot even be access-concentration (upacāra-samadhi) nor can there be the attainment of jhāna.

The Visuddhimagga (XII, 8) explains how difficult even the preliminary work is, and how difficult access-concentration and jhāna are. We read about each stage: "One in a hundred or thousand can do it." If one leads a worldly life and is busy with one's daily tasks there are no favourable conditions for jhāna. One cannot expect to attain jhāna if one just for a little while every day concentrates on breathing. Moreover, it is not concentration which should be stressed but right understanding, paññā. There must be right understanding of breath which is rūpa, conditioned by citta. It appears at the nose-tip or upper-lip, but it is very subtle. We should remember that mindfulness of breathing is one of the most difficult subjects of meditation.

We read in the Visuddhimagga (VIII, 211):

> '... But this mindfulness of breathing is difficult, difficult to develop, a field in which only the minds of Buddhas, Pacceka Buddhas, and Buddhas' sons are at home. It is no trivial matter, nor can it be cultivated by trivial persons...'

Buddhas' sons were the great disciples who had accumulated excellent qualities and skill for jhāna. Who can pretend to be among them? Mindfulness of breathing is a meditation subject of samatha and it is also included in one of the Four Applications of Mindfulness, Satipaṭṭhāna, under the section of Mindfulness of the Body. Thus, it can be applied in samatha and in vipassanā. We have to study this subject very carefully in order to avoid misunderstandings. The Visuddhimagga (Chapter VIII, 145-146) quotes the sutta about mindfulness of breathing in the Kindred Sayings (V, Mahā-vagga, Book X, Chapter I, §I). This sutta also occurs in other parts of the Tipiṭaka. I will quote the sutta text and then refer to the word commentary of the Visuddhimagga, in order that this sutta will be more clearly understood. We should note that there is a division into four sections of four clauses each in this sutta which, in the Visuddhimagga, are marked from I-XVI. The sutta states:

It has been described by the Blessed One as having sixteen bases thus: 'And how developed, bhikkhus, how practised much is concentration through mindfulness of breathing both peaceful and sublime, an unadulterated blissful abiding, banishing at once and stilling evil unprofitable thoughts as soon as they arise?

> Here, bhikkhus, a bhikkhu, gone to the forest or to the root of a tree or to an empty place, sits down; having folded his legs crosswise, set his body erect, established mindfulness in front of him, ever mindful he breathes in, mindful he breathes out. (I) Breathing in long, he knows "I breathe in long"; or breathing out long, he knows "I breathe out long".
>
> (II) Breathing in short, he knows "I breathe in short"; or breathing out short, he knows "I breathe out short". (III) He trains thus "I shall breathe in experiencing the whole body"; he trains thus "I shall breathe out experiencing the whole body". (IV) He trains thus "I shall breathe in tranquillizing the bodily activity"; he trains thus "I shall breathe out tranquillizing the bodily activity". (V) He trains thus "I shall breathe in experiencing happiness"; he trains thus "I shall breathe out experiencing happiness". (VI) He trains thus "I shall breathe in experiencing bliss"; he trains thus "I shall breathe out experienc-

ing bliss". (VII) He trains thus "I shall breathe in experiencing the mental formation"; he trains thus "I shall breathe out experiencing the mental formation". (VIII) He trains thus "I shall breathe in tranquillizing the mental formation"; he trains thus "I shall breathe out tranquillizing the mental formation". (IX) He trains thus "I shall breathe in experiencing the (manner of) consciousness"; he trains thus "I shall breathe out experiencing the (manner of) consciousness". (X) He trains thus "I shall breathe in gladdening the (manner of) consciousness"; he trains thus "I shall breathe out gladdening the (manner of) consciousness". (XI) He trains thus "I shall breathe in concentrating the (manner of) consciousness"; he trains thus "I shall breathe out concentrating the (manner of) consciousness". (XII) He trains thus "I shall breathe in liberating the (manner of) consciousness"; he trains thus "I shall breathe out liberating the (manner of) consciousness".

(XIII) He trains thus "I shall breathe in contemplating impermanence"; he trains thus "I shall breathe out contemplating impermanence". (XIV) He trains thus "I shall breathe in contemplating fading away"; he trains thus "I shall breathe out contemplating fading away". (XV) He trains thus "I shall breathe in contemplating cessation"; he trains thus "I shall breathe out contemplating cessation". (XVI) He trains thus "I shall breathe in contemplating relinquishment"; he trains thus "I shall breathe out contemplating relinquishment".

The Visuddhimagga (VIII, 186) describes the procedure of someone who wants to develop mindfulness of breathing until he has attained the fourth jhāna, and who then develops insight and through insight based on the fourth jhāna attains arahatship. We should not misunderstand the words "insight based on the fourth jhāna". It does not mean that he can forego the different stages of insight-knowledge, starting with the "defining of materiality–mentality" (nāma-rūpa pariccheda-ñāṇa), which is knowing the difference between the characteristic of nāma and the characteristic of rūpa. For example, when there is hearing there is sound as well, but their characteristics are different and they can only be known one at a time. Right understanding of the reality appearing at the present moment should be developed until there is no longer confusion as to the difference between the characteristics of nāma and rūpa. So long as this stage of insight has not been reached yet we are not sure whether the reality which appears at the present moment is nāma or rūpa.

Someone said that if one continues to concentrate on breathing the day will come when one realizes that this body is supported by mere breathing and that it perishes when breathing ceases. He said that in that way one fully realizes impermanence. However, the impermanence of conditioned realities will not be realized if the right cause has not been cultivated: awareness and understanding of different kinds of nāma and rūpa as they present themselves one at a time through the six doors.

Those who develop both jhāna and vipassanā should, after the jhānacitta has fallen away, be aware of nāma and rūpa, clearly know their different characteristics and develop all stages of insight (Visuddhimagga VIII, 223 and following). It depends on the accumulated wisdom whether the different stages of insight can be realized within a short time or whether they are developed very gradually during a long period of time. In the word commentary to the above quoted sutta the Visuddhimagga (VIII, 223-226) mentions with regard to the first tetrad (group of four clauses, marked I-IV) of the sutta the different stages of insight-knowledge which are developed after emerging from jhāna. We read:

78 CHAPTER 7. CONCENTRATION ON BREATHING

> 'After he has thus reached the four noble paths in due succession and has become established in the fruition of arahatship, he at last attains to the nineteen kinds of "Reviewing Knowledge", and he becomes fit to receive the highest gifts from the world with its deities.'

It is evident that only those who had accumulated great wisdom could attain jhāna with "mindfulness of breathing" as meditation subject, and then attain arahatship. This is beyond the capacity of ordinary people.

As regards the second tetrad (marked V-VIII), the Visuddhimagga (VIII, 226) comments:

> '(V) He trains thus "I shall breathe in... shall breathe out experiencing happiness", that is, making happiness (pīti, also translated as rapture) known, making it plain. Herein, the happiness is experienced in two ways: (a) with the object, and (b) with non-confusion.'

As regards "happiness experienced with the object", the Visuddhimagga (VIII, 227) explains:

> 'How is happiness experienced with the object? He attains the two jhānas in which happiness (pīti) is present. At the time when he has actually entered upon them the happiness is experienced with the object owing to the obtaining of the jhāna, because of the experiencing of the object.'

After the jhānacitta has fallen away paññā realizes the characteristic of pīti as it is: only a kind of nāma, which is impermanent and not self. We read:

> '...How with non-confusion? When, after entering upon and emerging from one of the two jhānas accompanied by pīti, he comprehends with insight that

happiness associated with the jhāna as liable to destruction and fall, then at the actual time of insight the happiness is experienced with non-confusion owing to the penetration of its characteristics (of impermanence, and so on).

In a similar way the words of the second tetrad are explained: "(VI) I shall breathe in... breathe out experiencing bliss (sukha)..." Sukha occurs in three stages of jhāna (of the fourfold system); it does not arise in the highest stage of jhāna where there is equanimity instead of sukha. Sukha accompanies the jhānacitta of the three stages of jhāna and is, after the jhānacitta has fallen away, realized by paññā as impermanent.

As regards the words in the third tetrad: "(X) I shall breathe in... breathe out gladdening the (manner of) consciousness", the Visuddhimagga (VIII, 231) states that there is gladdening in two ways, namely through concentration and through insight. We read:

> 'How through concentration? He attains the two jhānas in which happiness is present. At the time when he has actually entered upon them he inspires the mind with gladness, instils gladness into it, by means of the happiness associated with the jhāna. How through insight? After entering upon and emerging from one of the two jhānas accompanied by happiness he comprehends with insight that happiness associated with the jhāna as liable to destruction and to fall, thus at the actual time of insight he inspires the mind with gladness, instils gladness into it by making the happiness associated with jhāna the object.'

As regards the clause: "(XII) I shall breathe in... breathe out liberating the (manner of) consciousness", the Visuddhimagga explains that this also must be understood as pertaining to jhāna as well as to insight. In the first jhāna one is liberated from the "hindrances", although they are not eradicated, and in each subsequent stage of jhāna one is liberated from the jhāna-factors, specific cetasikas which are developed in order to eliminate the hindrances. The jhāna-factors are subsequently abandoned when one is no longer dependent on them and one is able to attain a higher and more subtle stage of jhāna. After emerging from jhāna the jhānacitta is comprehended with insight.

We read (Visuddhimagga VIII, 233):

> '... at the actual time of insight he delivers, liberates the mind from the perception of permanence by means of the contemplation of impermanence, from the perception of pleasure by means of the contemplation of dukkha (suffering), from the perception of self by means of the contemplation of not self...'

As regards the words of the fourth tetrad, "(XIII) I shall breathe in... breathe out contemplating impermanence", the Visuddhimagga (VIII, 234) states:

> '... Impermanence is the rise and fall and change in those same khandhas, or it is their non-existence after having been; the meaning is, it is the break-up of produced khandhas through their momentary dissolution since they do not remain in the same mode. Contemplation of impermanence is contemplation of materiality, etc., as "impermanent" in virtue of that impermanence...'

Further on the Visuddhimagga (VIII, 237) states about the fourth tetrad,

> 'This tetrad deals only with pure insight while the previous three deal with serenity and insight.'

As regards the clause: "(XIV) I shall breathe in... breathe out contemplating fading away", the Visuddhimagga states that there are two kinds of fading away, namely: "fading away as destruction" which is the "momentary dissolution of formations" (conditioned realities) and "absolute fading away" which is nibbāna. The text (Visuddhimagga VIII, 235) states:

'... Contemplation of fading away is insight and it is the path, which occur as the seeing of these two. It is when he possesses this twofold contemplation that it can be understood of him "He trains thus, I shall breathe in... shall breathe out contemplating fading away." '

The same method of explanation is applied to the clause "contemplating cessation". And with regard to the clause (XVI) "contemplating relinquishment", the Visuddhimagga states:

"relinquishment is of two kinds too, that is to say, relinquishment as giving up, and relinquishment as entering into."

"Giving up" is the giving up of defilements, and "entering into" is the entering into nibbāna, the Visuddhimagga explains. Also this clause pertains to insight alone. It is extremely difficult to develop jhāna and we should not think that it will be easier to develop insight if one tries to develop jhāna first. In the following sutta we read about "canker-destruction" depending on jhāna. It is clearly explained in what sense we should understand this. We read in the Gradual Sayings (Book of the Nines, Chapter VI, §5, Musing):

'Verily, monks, I say canker-destruction depends on the first jhāna ("musing")... And wherefore is this said? Consider the monk who, aloof from sense-desires... enters and abides in the first jhāna: whatever occurs there of rūpa, feeling, perception, activities (saṅkhāra) or consciousness, he sees wholly as impermanent phenomena, as ill, as a disease, a boil, a sting, a hurt, an affliction, as something alien, gimcrack, empty, not the self. He turns his mind away from such phenomena and, having done so, brings the mind towards the deathless element with the thought:

"This is the peace, this the summit, just this: the stilling of all mind-activity, the renouncing of all (rebirth) basis, the destroying of craving, passionless, ending, the cool." And steadfast therein he wins to canker-destruction; if not... just by reason of that Dhamma zest, that Dhamma sweetness, he snaps the five lower fetters and is born spontaneously and, being not subject to return from that world, becomes completely cool there.'

The same is said with regard to the other stages of jhāna. There can be no "canker-destruction", even for those who develop jhāna, unless the five khandhas, the conditioned nāmas and rūpas, are known as they are. Are there not five khandhas now, no matter what kind of citta arises, be it kusala citta or akusala citta? When something hard impinges on the bodysense, are there not five khandhas? Do we know already the difference between hardness and the nāma which experiences hardness? Hardness could not appear if there were no nāma which experiences it. It is not self who experiences it. Do we know the characteristic of painful feeling when it appears and the characteristic of aversion towards the pain? Different realities appear one at a time and when there is mindfulness they can be known as they are. Later on they can be realized as impermanent and not self. We should not forget that each moment of right understanding now eventually leads to "the destroying of craving, passionless, ending, the cool." It leads to "canker-destruction".

With mettā

Nina van Gorkom

8
Mindfulness of breathing

Tokyo
May 25
1971

Dear Mr. G.,

In my previous letter I quoted the sutta on Mindfulness of Breathing in the Kindred Sayings (V) and the word commentary of the Visuddhimagga, I will now continue with this subject. In the "Discourse on Mindfulness of Breathing" in the Middle Length Sayings (III, 118) we read that mindfulness of breathing, when developed, brings to fulfilment the four applications of mindfulness. The four applications of mindfulness are mindfulness of the body, of feelings, of cittas and of dhammas. We read:

> 'And how, monks, when mindfulness of in-breathing and out-breathing is developed, how when it is made much of, does it bring the four applications of mindfulness to fulfilment? At the time, monks, when a monk breathing in...
> breathing out a long breath... a short breath comprehends, "I am breathing in... breathing out a long breath... a short breath"; when he trains himself, thinking, "I will breathe in... breathe out experiencing the whole body... tranquillizing the activity of the body," at that time, monks, the monk is faring along contemplating the body in the body, ardent, clearly conscious (of it), mindful (of it) so as to control the covetousness and dejection in the world... the monk trains himself, thinking, "I will breathe in experiencing rapture (pīti)... I will breathe out experiencing rapture... I will breathe in... breathe out experiencing joy (sukha) ... I will breathe in... breathe out experiencing the activity of thought... I will breathe in... breathe out tranquillizing the activity of thought"; at that time, monks, the monk is faring along contemplating the feelings in the feelings, ardent, clearly conscious (of them), mindful (of them) so as to control the covetousness and dejection in the world...'

We then read that the monk, when he is developing mindfulness of breathing, contemplates citta in citta and dhamma in dhamma. Further on we read that the four applications of mindfulness bring the seven enlightenment factors to fulfilment. The seven enlightenment factors bring to fulfilment freedom through knowledge.

From the quotations of the Visuddhimagga in my previous letter we have seen that those who first develop samatha to the degree of jhāna and then develop insight, still have to be aware, after they emerge from jhāna, of the realities which appear. They should, for example, realize the rapture and joy experienced in jhāna, as only nāmas which are impermanent and not self. If one develops insight "based on jhāna", one should have the "fivefold mastery" (Visuddhimagga IV, 131), one should be able to attain jhāna and emerge from it at any time and in any place. Then the jhānacitta is for such a person a reality which naturally appears in his daily life. Only thus can it be object of mindfulness.

The Buddha encouraged people to be mindful while walking, eating, talking, in short, while doing all the things they would normally do. He did not say that samatha is a necessary requirement for the development of vipassanā. To those who had accumulated great wisdom and skill and who were inclined to the development of mindfulness of breathing, he explained how the development of this subject could bear great fruit, how it could bring the four applications of mindfulness to fulfilment. In being aware of nāma and rūpa one will learn to see the body in the body, feelings in the feelings, citta in citta and dhamma in dhamma. One will realize nāma and rūpa as not self. Then the four applications of mindfulness will be brought to fulfilment.

Samatha and vipassanā are two different ways of mental development, bhāvanā. The aim of samatha is to eliminate attachment to sense objects, and the aim of vipassanā is to eradicate ignorance of realities. Some people want to apply themselves to samatha first, because they think that in this way vipassanā can be developed more quickly afterwards. They should realize, however, that both samatha and vipassanā are ways of mental development. The Pāli term bhāvanā means: to make become, to produce, to increase. Developing first samatha before vipassanā is certainly not a "short cut" to nibbāna as some people believe. Those who want to develop samatha should do so only if they really have accumulated skill for samatha. If one wants to apply oneself to a meditation subject, one needs a great deal of preparation, one has to lead a secluded life and many conditions have to be fulfilled. Right understanding of the way to develop calm with the meditation subject is essential. If one just sits without any understanding, is that mental development? For the attainment of "access-concentration" and jhāna one needs perseverance with the development and one has to acquire great skill. Samatha, when it is really developed, is a way of kusala which is of a high degree. Jhāna purifies the mind, but the latent tendencies of defilements are not eradicated. After the jhānacitta has fallen away defilements are bound to arise again. As we have seen, those who have attained jhāna should still develop all the stages of insight in order to become enlightened.

One may apply oneself to samatha, but if one does not have accumulations for the attainment of jhāna, or even access concentration, one should consider for oneself whether it is beneficial or not to continue developing samatha. Even while one applies oneself to a meditation subject akusala cittas still arise; the hindrances are not suppressed until one has attained access-concentration and jhāna.

Vipassanā is to be developed in our daily life. If it is not developed in daily life we will not come to know our accumulated inclinations. Also our defilements should be known as they are, as conditioned nāmas, otherwise they cannot be eradicated. Vipassanā leads eventually to the eradication of defilements. It leads to the "ariyan calm" which is the highest degree of calm. We read in the "Discourse on the Analysis of the Elements" (Middle Length Sayings III, number. 140):

> "For this, monks, is the highest ariyan calm, that is to say the calm with regard to attachment, hatred and ignorance..."

It is still felt by some that if they apply themselves to samatha, even if they have not accumulated skill for jhāna, it would help them with the development of vipassanā. If one wants to use samatha as a way to attain enlightenment more quickly one should consider whether this is motivated by lobha or not. We should also know that sati and paññā in samatha are different from sati and paññā in vipassanā. In samatha there should be mindfulness and right understanding of the meditation subject and paññā should know when there is true calm, freedom from akusala. In vipassanā there is mindfulness of the nāma or rūpa which appears at the present moment through one of the six doors, so that paññā can realize them as not self. If one confuses the different ways of development of samatha and vipassanā, there will not be right understanding of cause and effect. One may erroneously think that the development of samatha is the way to obtain a great deal of sati of the Eightfold Path.

It is understandable that those who are discouraged about their akusala cittas and lack of mindfulness want to make special efforts to cause mindfulness to arise more frequently. As you wrote in your letter, you thought that concentration on breathing was for you the right condition for mindfulness of the Eightfold Path. You found that after this exercise the six doors were wide open; seeing and hearing seemed so clear. You felt like a spider in a web, ready to catch.

If there is mindfulness right now of, for example, sound or hardness, what is the condition for mindfulness? Is it necessary to concentrate on breathing first, in order to become more relaxed? We should remember the sutta in which are mentioned the four conditions, necessary for the attainment of the first stage of enlightenment, the stage of the sotāpanna (stream winner). We read in the Kindred Sayings (V, Mahā-vagga, Book XI, Kindred Sayings on Stream winning, Chapter I, §5) that the Buddha said to Sāriputta:

> ' "A limb of stream-winning! A limb of stream-winning!" is the saying, Sāriputta. Tell me, Sāriputta, of what sort is a limb of stream-winning? Lord, asso-

ciation with the upright is a limb of stream-winning.
Hearing the good Dhamma is a limb of stream-winning.
Applying the mind is a limb of stream-winning. Conforming to the Dhamma is a limb of stream-winning
Well said, Sāriputta! Well said, Sāriputta! Indeed
these are limbs of stream-winning...'

If we had not met the right person and listened to the Dhamma, if mindfulness of nāma and rūpa had not been explained to us, could there be "applying the mind", which is "wise consideration", and "conforming to the Dhamma", which is the development of the Eightfold Path? Could there be awareness of nāma and rūpa, right at this moment? Mindfulness and understanding are still weak, but, when one has listened to the Dhamma, there can be a beginning of the study of different realities which appear.

You felt like a spider in a web, ready to catch. When there is a thought of catching realities, there is a concept of self. Realities appear and if there are conditions for mindfulness it arises. It may arise or it may not, this does not depend on a self. Seeing and hearing seemed so clear to you. When are these realities clear? Only when paññā realizes the characteristics of seeing and hearing as not self, not when we have a sensation that they are clear. Can we say that anything is clear when we do not even know the difference between seeing and visible object, hearing and sound?

You thought that after concentration on breathing, when you were relaxed, awareness was frequent and acute. How much understanding is there? Which realities are understood? If there is no right understanding we may take for awareness what is not the right awareness. The realities which appear through the six doors at this moment have to be understood. They cannot be understood immediately, but we can begin to study them with awareness. Is there not something which appears through the eyes now? We do not have to think about it or to define it in order to experience it. We can call it visible object or colour, it does not matter how we name it; it is just that which appears through the eyes. When we think that it is a particular person or thing, we are thinking of concepts. A concept is not visible object, it is formed up by our thinking. A concept is not a reality and thus it is not the object of right understanding in the development of vipassanā.

Do we know the difference between concepts and nāma and rūpa, the realities which can be directly experienced, without there being the need to think about them? It is essential to know the difference, otherwise we will continue confusing thinking and awareness, and then vipassanā cannot be developed. When visible object appears it is evident that there must also be a reality which experiences it, otherwise it could not appear. Seeing which experiences visible object is not self, it is only a type of nāma. Seeing can be studied with mindfulness when there is seeing, and there is seeing time and again. There is seeing now. We used to live in the world of our thoughts, of concepts, but now we can begin to study realities such as seeing, visible object, hearing or sound. We are not used to doing this but when we see the value of knowing what is real, not a concept or idea, there will be conditions to study realities. We are ignorant about all the realities of our daily life. It seems to us that there are seeing and thinking about what is seen at the same time, but in reality they are different realities arising at different moments. Do we realize this? It seems to us that there are hearing and thinking of the meaning of what is heard at the same time but they are different realities. When we do not clearly distinguish between different realities, can we say that any reality is clearly understood? If there is still doubt it is evident that paññā is weak. It is beneficial to realize what one does not know yet.

Ignorance and doubt can only be very gradually eliminated through the development of paññā which directly knows nāma and rūpa. We may not be aware of one object at a time yet, there may be a notion of self who is watching realities. When there is an idea of "watching" we are not on the right path. Realities such as hardness or sound appear already, because of their own conditions. They can be studied with mindfulness which also arises because of its own conditions, namely, as we have seen, listening to the Dhamma and considering it. When we remember that the realities which appear one at a time have to be studied in order to have more understanding of them, there will be less worry about the frequency of sati. If one erroneously believes that nāma and rūpa are known already there is no development of paññā. When there is right mindfulness realities appear one at a time and there is no self who is watching.

If there cannot be awareness of all kinds of nāma and rūpa which appear in our daily life, no matter whether we are busy or agitated, we will not really know ourselves. If we think that we have to be relaxed first we limit the objects of awareness. The development of paññā should be very natural. There should be no excitement about awareness, no thoughts about its frequency or acuteness. Is there still doubt about the reality which appears now? If there is awareness doubt can gradually be eliminated. If one believes that one has to calm down first before there can be awareness there cannot be awareness of whatever reality naturally appears. If the development of paññā is not natural one hinders its development.

If you are inclined to concentrate on breathing when you are agitated or have aversion, it would be very helpful if you could be aware of realities appearing at such moments. Are there not akusala cittas and should these realities not be known? When you wish to become relaxed through concentration on breathing is there no attachment? It is a reality and it can be object of mindfulness. Are there not different feelings: pleasant feeling, unpleasant feeling and indifferent feeling? These can be object of mindfulness. If there can be awareness when you feel tense you can find out that there are nāmas and rūpas at such moments. Insight can only be developed if there is mindfulness of any reality which appears. If you believe that there cannot be awareness of aversion this reality will not be known as only a nāma, arising because of conditions. If there can be awareness in your daily life you will start to know yourself. You will be able to find out whether concentration on breathing is beneficial or not, whether it helps you to develop right understanding or not.

When there are many akusala cittas we may be inclined to look for a way to eliminate them quickly. Those who think that they want to apply themselves to samatha in order to have less akusala cittas, should find out whether they really have accumulations to develop samatha and whether the circumstances of their lives are such that the conditions which are necessary for its development can be fulfilled. It is important to know which cause brings which effect in life. If samatha is developed in the right way and jhāna can be attained, there will be the temporary elimination of defilements. If jhānacitta can arise shortly before dying there will be a happy rebirth in a higher plane of existence. However, the development of jhāna, as we have seen, is extremely difficult and very few people can do it. One may take for jhāna what is merely an unusual experience, not jhāna. Even if one develops samatha in the right way and one attains jhāna, one still has to develop insight in order to become detached from the concept of self and in order that all latent tendencies of defilements can be eradicated. Jhāna can lead to a happy rebirth, but vipassanā can lead to the end of birth, to the end of dukkha. The growth of insight knowledge cannot be forced, it has to be developed stage by stage. We read in the Kindred Sayings (IV, Saḷāyatana-vagga, Kindred Sayings on Sense, Second Fifty, Chapter III, §74, Sick) that the Buddha visited a sick monk, who said that he did not understand the meaning of the purity of life in the Dhamma taught by the Buddha. When the Buddha asked him in what sense he understood it, he answered:

> "Passion and the destruction of passion, lord,–that is what I understand to be the Dhamma taught by the Exalted One."
>
> "Well said, monk! Well said! Well indeed do you understand the meaning of the Dhamma taught by me. Indeed it means passion and the destruction of passion.
>
> Now what think you, monk? Is the eye permanent or impermanent?" "Impermanent, lord."
>
> "Is the ear... nose... tongue... body... is mind permanent or impermanent?"
>
> "Impermanent, lord."
>
> "And what is impermanent, is that happiness or dukkha (suffering)?"
>
> "Dukkha, lord."
>
> "And what is impermanent, dukkha, by nature changeable,–is it proper to regard that as 'This is mine. I am this. This is myself'?"
>
> "No, indeed, lord."
>
> "If he sees thus, the well-taught ariyan disciple is repelled by the eye, the ear, the tongue... so that he realizes 'For life in these conditions there is no hereafter.' "
>
> 'Thus spoke the Exalted One. And that monk was delighted and welcomed the words of the Exalted One. Moreover, when this discourse was uttered, in that monk arose the pure and flawless eye of the Dhamma, (so that he saw) "Whatsoever is of a nature to arise, all that is of a nature to cease." '

For the sick monk the four necessary conditions for enlightenment were fulfilled: he had met the right person, he had listened to the Dhamma which was explained to him, he had wisely considered it and he had developed right understanding of realities. Should we be surprised that the Buddha, in order to show the way to the destruction of passion, first asked: "Is the eye permanent or impermanent?". And the same for the other doorways? People who wish to get rid of passion quickly may wonder whether they should suppress it, rather than develop understanding of realities appearing through the six doors. The development of understanding seems to be a long way to get rid of passion. However, the Buddha showed cause and effect. There cannot be the destruction of passion without there being first the eradication of the wrong view of self through awareness of all realities which appear. When right understanding of nāma and rūpa has been developed they can be realized as impermanent and not self. This is the only way that leads to detachment from the eye, the ear, the nose, the tongue, the body, the mind, to detachment from all realities. Realities appearing through the six doors are explained in the Tipiṭaka time and again, and whenever we read about this we can be reminded to be aware right at that moment. Are there not phenomena appearing through the six doors all the time? We should not be forgetful of them so that the way leading to enlightenment can be realized.

With mettā,

Nina van Gorkom

9
Doing complicated things

Tokyo
June 15
1971

Dear Mr. G.,

You found it difficult to be aware while doing complicated things. I will quote from your letter:
'When I do things which can be performed automatically, like shaving, eating and walking, there can be awareness. But when I do complicated things like remembering a combination of numbers in order to open a safe, there cannot be awareness. I find that a special effort is needed for awareness of nāma and rūpa. While I have to exert myself to do complicated things I

have no energy left for awareness. When I, for example, study a foreign language and I make an effort to memorize the words, I exclude all other things from my mind. At such moments I could not be aware.'

Shaving, walking, eating, opening a safe, all these things we can do because there are conditions to be able to do them. If you had not been taught you would not know how to open a safe. Remembering something is nāma, arising because of conditions. If we forget something, that also depends on conditions. The more we understand that realities are only nāma and rūpa, arising because of their own conditions, the less will there be hindrances to awareness. Realities such as visible object, hardness or feeling arise already because of their own conditions and you can begin to consider their different characteristics. You should not think of having to make an effort for sati because then there is still a notion of self who is aware. Sati can arise naturally in your daily life. When there is the study with awareness of one reality at a time there is a beginning of understanding. One should not try to hold on to realities in order to study them, because they do not stay.

We believe that realities are the way we experience them, but in fact we experience them in a distorted way. It seems to us that realities such as hardness or visible object stay because their arising and falling away has not been realized yet. Their impermanence cannot be realized so long as paññā has not yet been developed to that stage. We know in theory that there is no self, but we still cling to the idea of self who is aware. We may take energy or effort for self. Effort or energy (viriya) is a cetasika, a mental factor which arises with many cittas, though not with each type. It arises with the citta and falls away together with it. When it accompanies kusala citta it is kusala and when it accompanies akusala citta it is akusala. There is no self who can exert control over effort, who can cause it to be kusala. When there is right awareness of a nāma or rūpa which appears through one of the six doors, there is already right effort accompanying the kusala citta. We do not have to try or to think of effort. When there is still wrong view, we may think that we cannot be aware while doing complicated things. We may think that at such moments awareness is more difficult than when we are walking or doing things which do not require much attention. In reality there is no difference. If one believes that there is a difference, one does not know what right awareness is. If there is less of a preconceived idea that in particular situations awareness is impossible, there can be awareness also while doing complicated things. We may be absorbed in what we are doing, but that doesn't matter. Being absorbed is a reality, it can be known as only a type of nāma. Realities appear already because of their own conditions, and gradually we can learn to study their characteristics.

Misunderstandings are bound to arise as to what awareness really is and because of these misunderstandings people think that it is impossible to be aware in daily life. Someone wrote, for instance, that awareness is the same as keeping oneself under constant observation. We should observe ourselves in action, he said, and this can be done quite simply by asking oneself, "What am I doing?". He thought that in this way we learn to be aware of what we are doing and that this constitutes awareness.

The word awareness in conventional language has a meaning which is different from awareness, sati, of the Eightfold Path. When we ask ourselves, "What am I doing?", what is the reality at that moment? There are many types of citta which think at such moments. If we do not realize that it is nāma which thinks while we ask ourselves, "What am I doing?", the wrong view of self will not be eradicated. There is only thinking about the self who is performing different actions. There is no sati of the Eightfold Path, there is no development of understanding of the different characteristics of nāma and rūpa. When we are reading and we answer the question, "What am I doing?", with, "I am reading", without development of understanding, we live only in the world of conventional truth. We will continue to be ignorant of the absolute truth, the truth about nāma and rūpa. When we are reading, is there not the nāma which experiences visible object, is there not the rūpa which is visible object, is there not the nāma which thinks about the meaning of what is read, and should these realities not be known? It is the same when we are walking, talking or eating, if we only know "I am walking, talking and eating", it is not at all helpful for the development of paññā. There is still the wrong view of self. While we are walking, talking and eating there are nāma and rūpa appearing through the six doors, and right understanding can be developed of them. Some people believe that they have to slow down all their movements in order to be able to be aware. Is there desire for awareness? If one is not aware naturally in one's daily life paññā cannot develop. The "Satipaṭṭhāna sutta" (Middle Length Sayings I, no. 10) reminds us to be aware in our daily life, no matter what we are doing.

We read under the section of mindfulness of the body, regarding the postures:

> 'And again, monks, a monk, when he is walking, comprehends, "I am walking"; or when he is standing still, comprehends, "I am standing still"; or when he is sitting down, comprehends, "I am sitting down"; or when he is lying down, comprehends, "I am lying down". So that however his body is disposed he comprehends that it is like that. Thus he fares along contemplating the body in the body internally, or he fares along contemplating the body in the body externally, or he fares along contemplating the body in the body internally and externally...'

The commentary to this sutta, the "Papañcasūdani" explains the words, "When he is going, a monk understands 'I am going'

" as follows:

> 'In this matter of going, readily do dogs, jackals and the like, know when they move on that they are moving. But this instruction on the modes of deportment was not given concerning similar awareness, because awareness of that sort belonging to animals does not shed the belief in a living being, does not knock out the perception of a soul and neither becomes a subject of meditation nor the development of satipaṭṭhāna.'

The commentary explains that there is no living being. There is going on account of the diffusion of the process of oscillation (motion) born of mental activity. There are only nāma and rūpa which arise because of conditions. When the monk is walking, standing, sitting or lying down, he contemplates the body in the body, he does not take the body for self. He is mindful of the realities which appear.

We read in the following section of the sutta, the section on clear comprehension:

> 'And again, monks, a monk when he is setting out or returning is one acting in a clearly conscious way; when he is looking in front or looking around... when he has bent in or stretched out (his arm)... when he is carrying his outer cloak, bowl and robe... when he is obeying the calls of nature... when he is walking, standing, sitting, asleep, awake, talking, silent, he is one acting in a clearly conscious way.
>
> Thus he fares along contemplating the body in the body internally... externally... internally and externally...'

If one thinks of the body as a "whole" the arising and falling away of rūpas cannot be realized and one will continue to cling to the idea of "my body". During all one's activities there can be the development of right understanding, so that wrong view can be eradicated.

Sati is not: observing oneself in action. Sati arises with each "beautiful" (sobhana) citta and its function is being non-forgetful of what is wholesome. Sati is different from the cetasika saññā, remembrance or "perception", which arises with each citta. Saññā recognizes or "marks" the object, so that it can be recognized later on. Sati of the Eightfold Path is mindful of the reality which presents itself at the present moment, and then right understanding of it can be developed. We do not have to think of sati, it arises when there are conditions for it. When right understanding of a reality which presents itself is being developed, there is also sati which is mindful, non-forgetful, of that reality. For example, when the characteristic of hardness appears and it is realized as a kind of rūpa, it is evident that there is sati. When we think, "I am eating" and we are not aware of different nāmas and rūpas which appear, there is a concept of self who is eating. When right understanding is developed the "self" is broken up into different nāma-elements and rūpa-elements. In order that right understanding can be developed there should be mindfulness of a characteristic of nāma or rūpa, not mindfulness without knowing anything.

If one thinks that sati means keeping oneself under constant observation, one is bound to believe that it is impossible to be aware while doing things which require special attention. One may be urged to make special efforts in order to create conditions for a great deal of sati. Any speculation about creating conditions for the arising of sati distracts from the study of the reality appearing right at this moment. It is thinking of the future instead of being aware of aversion now, seeing now, thinking now. There is clinging to an idea of self who can control awareness, and in that way there will not be detachment from the concept of self.

If we understand more clearly that our life consists of nāma and rūpa which arise because of conditions, we will be less absorbed in the idea of self while we do complicated things. Also at such moments there are only nāma and rūpa. We may believe that while we are talking there cannot be awareness, since we have to think about what we are saying. There is sound and can there not be awareness of it? It is citta, not self, which thinks about what we are going to say and which conditions sound. There can be awareness of realities in between thinking. I noticed that while I am writing the Chinese script (Kanji), it is possible to hear other people talking or to think of other things. This shows that there are many different types of cittas which succeed one another so rapidly that it seems that they occur all at the same time. Since there can be hearing or thinking in between the writing of Kanji, there can also be awareness in between.

You mentioned that you could not be aware while learning a foreign language. Learning a foreign language can teach us about reality. When we learn a foreign language such as Japanese we cannot in the beginning translate quickly. Later on we acquire skill and it seems that we do it automatically. When we hear a Japanese word we immediately know the meaning, it seems that hearing and knowing the meaning occur at the same time. However, we know that they are different moments of citta. Also when we hear words spoken in our own language there is hearing and then "translating" going on, we interpret the sounds so that we understand the meaning. The process of translation goes on very rapidly, it goes on the whole day. When there is seeing, visible object is experienced, but immediately we translate what we see, we interpret it, and then we discern people and things. If we consider the process of translation we can understand more clearly that seeing and hearing are different from thinking. The moments that we do not translate seeing and hearing can be studied. Thus, no matter whether you learn a foreign language or whether you are merely thinking after seeing or hearing, there is translating going on time and again. No matter what we do, there are nāma and rūpa, and sometimes sati can arise and be aware of them. We cannot control the cittas which arise. They arise and perform their own functions. So long as we believe that we can create conditions for the arising of sati, the right awareness will not arise. One may believe that there is sati when there is only ignorance of realities. Awareness can arise if there are conditions for it. The conditions are listening to the Dhamma and considering it. We may believe that we have listened and considered enough, but, when there are still misunderstandings about the Eightfold Path it is evident that our listening and considering have not been enough. We should not assume too soon that we studied enough. We have accumulated ignorance for aeons and therefore it will take aeons before it can be eradicated. This should not discourage us, but we should continue to listen, to read and to study, and we should consider thoroughly what we learnt. We should consider the Dhamma with regard to our own experiences in daily life.

Rāhula, the Buddha's son, attained arahatship when he was only twenty years old. For him the conditions necessary for enlightenment were fulfilled: he associated with the right person, the Buddha, he listened to the Dhamma, he considered it and he developed the Eightfold Path. We read in the Middle Length Sayings (II, no. 62, "Greater Discourse on an Exhortation to Rāhula") that Rāhula asked the Buddha how mindfulness of breathing, when it is developed and made much of, is of great fruit, of great advantage. The Buddha did not speak immediately about mindfulness of breathing, he first taught Rāhula about the elements of solidity, cohesion, heat, motion and space. No matter whether these elements are internal or external, they should not be taken for self. The Buddha then said to Rāhula:

'Develop the mind-development that is like the earth,

Rāhula. For, from developing the mind-development that is like the earth, Rāhula, agreeable and disagreeable sensory impressions that have arisen, taking hold of your thought, will not persist.'

In the same way the Buddha told Rāhula to develop the mind- development that is like water, fire, wind and space (air). What are we doing when there are agreeable or disagreeable sense-impressions that take hold of us? Do we take them for self, or can we realize them as only elements? Rāhula had to be mindful of all realities appearing through the six doors in order to see them as only elements.

Further on we read that the Buddha encouraged Rāhula to the development of lovingkindness, compassion, sympathetic joy, equanimity, the contemplation of the foul and the perception of impermanence. It was only after the Buddha had taught all this to Rāhula that he spoke about mindfulness of breathing. Rāhula did not apply himself to this subject without knowing anything. While he applied himself to mindfulness of breathing he realized the true nature of all nāmas and rūpas appearing through the six doors. He had accumulated great wisdom and therefore he was able to develop mindfulness of breathing so that it was of great fruit, of great advantage. The Buddha said that if it was developed in that way the final in-breaths and out-breaths too are known as they cease, they are not unknown.

The Buddha taught Rāhula about the eye, visible object and seeing-consciousness, about all realities which appear through the six doors. He taught Rāhula until he attained arahatship. We read in the Kindred Sayings (IV, Saḷāyatana-vagga, Kindred Sayings on Sense, Third Fifty, Chapter II, §121, Rāhula) that it occurred to the Buddha, while he was near Sāvatthī, at the Jeta Grove, that Rāhula was ripe for the attainment of arahatship. He wanted to give Rāhula the last teachings and he said to him that they would go to Dark Wood. We read:

CHAPTER 9. DOING COMPLICATED THINGS

'Now at that time countless thousands of devas were following the Exalted One, thinking: "Today the Exalted One will give the venerable Rāhula the last teachings for the destruction of the āsavas."

So the Exalted One plunged into the depths of Dark Wood and sat down at the foot of a certain tree on the seat prepared for him. And the venerable Rāhula, saluting the Exalted One, sat down also at one side. As he thus sat the Exalted One said to the venerable Rāhula:

"Now what do you think, Rāhula? Is the eye permanent or impermanent?"

"Impermanent, lord."

"What is impermanent is that happiness or dukkha?"

"Dukkha, lord."

"Now what is impermanent, woeful, by nature changeable–is it fitting to regard that as 'This is mine. This am I. This is myself?' "

"Surely not, lord."

(The same is said about the other phenomena appearing through the sense-doors and through the mind-door.)

Thus spoke the Exalted One. And the venerable Rāhula was delighted with the words of the Exalted One and welcomed them. And when this instruction was given, the venerable Rāhula's heart was freed from the āsavas without grasping. And in those countless devas arose the pure and spotless eye of the Dhamma, so that they knew:

"Whatsoever is of a nature to arise, all that is of a nature to cease." '

When we read this sutta we may find it to be a repetition of so many suttas. We may read it countless times, but we may only have theoretical understanding of the truth. One day the truth may be realized but this depends on the degree of the development of paññā. Is the eye permanent or impermanent? Is what is impermanent happiness or dukkha? Should we take it for self? Are the other realities permanent or impermanent? The Buddha spoke about all the realities which appear now. If we do not yet have a keen understanding of seeing and visible object which appear now, at this moment, if we cannot yet distinguish between the different characteristics of nāma and of rūpa which appear now, their arising and falling away cannot be realized. When the Buddha asked Rāhula about the true nature of realities, would Rāhula only have been thinking about nāma and rūpa, or did he at that moment realize their true nature? We know the answer. Rāhula was mindful of realities appearing through the six doors, and thus his wisdom could be fully developed. Otherwise he could not have attained arahatship.

With mettā

Nina van Gorkom

10
Right awareness

Tokyo
July 15
1971

Dear Mr. G.,

You wrote: "When I am aware of nāma and rūpa, I find that their appearance is not always followed by wisdom about them." We are bound to have doubts about the characteristic of sati and the characteristic of paññā. Objects are experienced time and again without sati. We are absorbed in pleasant objects and we have aversion towards unpleasant objects; there are akusala cittas and there is no mindfulness of realities. Sometimes there can be conditions for awareness and then it arises just for a short moment. There can be "study" with awareness of realities, such as hardness which appears or feeling which presents itself. When there is the "study" of a characteristic of nāma or rūpa, there is a beginning of the development of paññā, although paññā is still weak. When you say that the appearance of nāma and rūpa is not always followed by paññā you assume that there is first aware-ness and that paññā follows later on. There can be sati without there being paññā at that moment, but then there is no development of the Eightfold Path. Sati accompanies each kusala citta and there are many levels of sati. When there is awareness of a characteristic of nāma or rūpa there is development of understanding of that characteristic right at that moment. Paññā of the Eightfold Path is not thinking about realities which have fallen away already.

Right awareness of the Eightfold Path is difficult. There has to be awareness of one nāma or rūpa, of one object at a time. Do realities appear one at a time? It seems that there can be seeing and hearing or seeing and thinking at the same time. We may have begun to study what appears through the eyes, visible object, but is the characteristic of seeing known already? The nāma which sees seems to be hidden, we cannot grasp it, it seems to escape us. It is only paññā which can know nāma and rūpa as they are. Don't we take the study of realities for self? Then we are on the wrong way and nāma and rūpa will not be known as they are. We have an idea that they escape us. So long as we are not sotāpanna we have to continue to take into account that we have wrong view and that we follow the wrong practice.

The development of the Eightfold Path is not different from developing understanding of the reality which appears right now. If there is awareness of visible object than that reality can be studied so that it can be known as only a rūpa. If seeing is not the object of awareness that reality cannot be studied and we should not try to be aware of it. It depends on paññā which types of realities are understood, it does not depend on us. When paññā grows there will be conditions that more types of realities will be known. There is hearing time and again, and we can learn that when there is hearing only sound is heard, that words cannot be heard. There is thinking when we distinguish different words and know their meaning. There can be a beginning of understanding of different characteristics and this is the development of the Eightfold Path. We should not worry about the moments of sati and paññā, but we should remember our goal: the understanding of realities which appear now.

You wrote that when you do gymnastic exercises you can experience the difference between motion and seeing the motion. When we speak about "seeing motion", what is the reality which can be experienced? What can be seen? Can motion be experienced through eye-sense? When we use the word motion in conventional language we think of a whole situation, of people or things which move. We believe that we can see people and things move. Through eyes only colour or visible object is experienced, but seeing conditions thinking of people and things which move. If there were not the experience of visible object we could not think about concepts of people and things which move. Saññā, remembrance, is the condition that we know that there are people and things and that we can observe their movements. As regards motion, this is a kind of rūpa, the element of wind, which has the characteristic of motion or pressure. This type of rūpa can be experienced through the body-sense. It is different from what we mean by motion in conventional language.

We think of a person who moves his body, but actually there is no person and there is not a body which stays. The body consists of the four Great Elements of Earth (solidity), Water (cohesion), Fire (temperature) and Wind (motion), and of other types of rūpas. The rūpas of the body arise and then fall away immediately. There is no living being who goes, but it is citta which conditions the movement of the rūpas we call "our body".

There can be awareness of different realities which appear one at a time. Through eyes only visible object appears, through body-sense hardness, softness, heat, cold, motion or pressure can appear. A concept of the whole body or of a person is not a reality, but the thinking of it is real, it is nāma. We may notice that there is thinking and just be satisfied to know that. We call it "thinking", but do we have right understanding of it? When there is thinking there are many different types of cittas, succeeding one another. Sometimes there are kusala cittas, but most of the time there are akusala cittas when we are thinking, cittas rooted in lobha, dosa and moha. We are inclined to take the different moments of thinking as a "whole", thinking seems to last. Do we cling to an idea of self who thinks? If we learn to be aware of nāma and rūpa as they present themselves one at a time, the self will begin to disintegrate.

Someone asked me: "How can we ever know different realities which succeed one another so quickly? Do we not have to be extremely fast?"

There is no self who knows realities, it is paññā which is able to know them. If we think that we have to be fast we cling to a concept of self and this hinders the development of right understanding. When there are conditions for the arising of awareness paññā will gradually develop and it will perform its function. We should consider the definition of paññā or non-delusion given in the Visuddhimagga (XIV, 143):

> 'Non-delusion has the characteristic of penetrating things according to their individual essences, or it has the characteristic of sure penetration, like the penetration of an arrow shot by a skilful archer. Its function is to illuminate the objective field, like a lamp. It is manifested as non-bewilderment, like a guide in a forest...'

When paññā has been developed it is as fast as an arrow shot by a skilful archer, and it is sure in its penetration of the true nature of realities. It illuminates the object which is experienced so that it is known as it really is. It is paññā, not self, which is so keen that it knows precisely the reality which appears as it is.

It is important to know when there is clinging to awareness, it may be so subtle that we do not notice it. The best cure is studying the reality which appears right now. Even clinging to awareness can be realized as a type of nāma. It arises because we have accumulated clinging.

When paññā has not been developed we have doubt about all the realities which appear. We do not know precisely when there is kusala citta, when akusala citta and when vipāka-citta, citta which is the result of kamma. Someone had a question about the nature of vipāka-citta: "Can we know when vipāka-citta is kusala vipāka, the result of kusala kamma, and when akusala vipāka, the result of akusala kamma? Can we know when the object which vipāka-citta experiences is a pleasant object and when an unpleasant object?"

We cannot always know whether an object is pleasant or unpleasant. Moreover, we may take for pleasant what is not pleasant, since we are attached to particular things with which we are familiar. When we see something there is visible object which impinges on the eye-sense. Seeing is vipāka-citta and it experiences only visible object. It does not experience things such as a house or a tree. Those are concepts which are experienced by cittas arising in a mind-door process. There are sense-door processes and mind-door processes succeeding one another very quickly. When we are looking at something there are eye-door processes and mind-door processes. Visible object impinges on the eye-door time and again and it is hard to tell when visible object which is pleasant and when visible object which is unpleasant impinges on the eye-sense. It is difficult to know which of the many moments of seeing and hearing are kusala vipāka and which akusala vipāka. Akusala vipāka and kusala vipāka arise in different processes of citta but cittas succeed one another so quickly that what are in fact countless cittas seem to be one moment.

We do not clearly distinguish between different realities, we "join" them together. When we think of vipāka, we usually think of a whole situation. For example we think that being in a swimmingpool is kusala vipāka and we cling to this situation. When I was swimming there was at one moment the experience of a pleasant object through the body-sense, at another moment an unpleasant object. When we enjoy doing something like swimming, we do not always notice it when the object which is experienced is unpleasant. The object is unpleasant when, for example, the temperature of the water is just a little too cold. We are ignorant of the realities which appear one at a time. Swimming pool is not a reality which can be directly experienced. Phenomena such as cold, softness, attachment or aversion are realities which can be directly experienced when they present themselves one at a time.

Vipāka is such a short moment, why should we try to find out whether it is kusala vipāka or akusala vipāka? When the vipāka has already fallen away we continue to think about it. We find it so important whether there is kusala vipāka or akusala vipāka in our life. We regret the days when there is a great deal of akusala vipāka and we think of a "self" who has to receive it. Vipāka is the result of kamma. It arises just for a moment and then it falls away. When we hear unpleasant words the experience of sound is a moment of vipāka and it falls away immediately. At the moment of hearing we do not know the meaning of the words yet. When we know the meaning there is thinking, and then there are usually akusala cittas which think with aversion about those words. We cannot change what has happened, but what can be done is the development of right understanding of realities. It is essential to know when there is kusala citta, when akusala citta and when vipāka-citta, but we should not try to find out whether the vipāka was kusala vipāka or akusala vipāka. Seeing, for example, is vipāka and after it has fallen away there are kusala cittas or akusala cittas, but most of the time there are akusala cittas. We are attached to visible object or we have aversion towards it. It is important to know these types of akusala cittas which arise after the vipāka-citta.

Someone asked me whether it is possible to have kusala cittas after akusala vipāka and akusala cittas after kusala vipāka. There can be kusala cittas after akusala vipāka and akusala cittas after kusala vipāka, because the conditions for these different types of cittas are entirely different. Vipāka-citta is the result of kamma, a deed committed in the past. Akusala cittas and kusala cittas are conditioned by our accumulations of akusala and kusala. I will give an example of an unpleasant object after the experience of which there can be different types of citta, kusala citta or akusala citta, depending on one's accumulations. If one sees a dead cat, different types of citta may arise on account of what is seen. We may think of the dead cat without awareness of realities and we may take the cat for "something" which stays. We may have aversion towards it. What is the dead cat? When we are looking there is visible object, when we touch it there is hardness or softness. Through the nose odour presents itself. It is because of saññā, remembrance, that a "whole", the dead cat, is remembered. In reality there is no dead cat, there are only different elements arising and falling away. Someone who has developed calm may have kusala cittas with calm when he sees a dead cat. He may take it as a meditation subject, the foulness of the body. He may remember that also his own body is subject to decay. If he has accumulated skill for jhāna, jhāna can be attained with this subject. Someone who develops vipassanā can be reminded of the true nature of realities, their nature of impermanence and anattā. He is aware of whatever nāma or rūpa presents itself at that moment in order to know realities as they are. He may even at that moment attain enlightenment. It all depends on one's accumulations whether there are, after having seen a foul object, akusala cittas, mahā-kusala citta (kusala cittas of the sense-sphere), jhāna-cittas or lokuttara cittas. The "cemetery-meditations" are included in the "Applications of Mindfulness", under the section of "Mindfulness of the Body". We read in the "Satipaṭṭhāna-sutta" (Middle Length Sayings I, no. 10):

> 'And again, monks, as a monk might see a body thrown aside in a cemetery, dead for one day or for two days or for three days, swollen, discoloured, decomposing; he focuses on this body itself, thinking: "This body, too, is of a similar nature, a similar constitution, it has not got past that (state of things)."... It is thus too, monks, that a monk fares along contemplating the body in the body.'

This passage can be applied by all who develop vipassanā, no matter whether they have first developed the "cemetery-meditations" as a meditation subject of samatha or not. What we take for our body are only elements which are each moment subject to decay. We should "contemplate the body in the body", we should not take it for something which stays, for "self".

In the Visuddhimagga (I, 55) we read about the monk Mahā Tissa who met a woman when he was walking in the village. When she was smiling he saw her teeth and attained arahatship. We read:

> It seems that while the Elder was going on his way from Cetiyapabbata to Anurādhapura for alms, a certain daughter-in-law of a clan, who had quarrelled with her husband and had set out early from Anurādhapura all dressed up and tricked out like a celestial nymph to go to her relatives' home, saw him on the road, and being low-minded, she laughed a

loud laugh. (Wondering) "What is that?", the Elder looked up, and finding in the bones of her teeth the perception of foulness (ugliness), he reached arahatship. Hence it was said:

'He saw the bones that were her teeth,
And kept in mind his first perception;
And standing on that very spot
The Elder became an arahat.'

But her husband who was going after her saw the Elder and asked, "Venerable sir, did you by any chance see a woman?" The Elder told him:

"Whether it was a man or woman
That went by I noticed not;
But only that on this high road
There goes a group of bones."

Did you note the Elder's answer? Was he attached to concepts such as "man", "woman"? Did he take what he perceived for self? He saw the body in the body; he was aware of realities. Because of his accumulated wisdom he did not take what he saw for a being, a "self"–he only saw a group of bones, something foul. How often do we take for beautiful what is foul. He realized nāma and rūpa as they are and attained arahatship.

Those who have developed both samatha and vipassanā may, when they have seen something foul, have jhānacittas which have foulness as their object. It depends on one's accumulations whether or not jhānacittas arise. But in order to know things as they are, one should see the body in the body, feelings in the feelings, citta in citta, dhamma in dhamma. In other words, one should realize the true nature of the reality which appears at this moment. The Visuddhimagga explains, just before the passage about Mahā Tissa, the virtue of restraint of the faculties (indriya-saṁvara-sīla). There is this kind of sīla when there is mindfulness of realities appearing through the six doors. When there is mindfulness and understanding of the objects experienced through the six doors these doors are "guarded" against akusala. The Visuddhimagga states: "He apprehends what is really there..." Do we "apprehend what is really there", or do we have wrong view? Do we take realities for permanent and for self instead of being mindful of them? We do not have to refrain from thinking about concepts but there can be less clinging to them. When we think of concepts such as "man" or "woman" we can remember that thinking is a reality which can be object of mindfulness. It is only a kind of nāma arising because of conditions, not self. It is because of saññā that we remember that this is a man and that a woman. Whatever reality is the object of mindfulness depends on sati, not on a self. The Elder, because of his accumulations, did not notice a woman, but there was the perception of foulness and then he realized things as they are. In that way he was not absorbed in the idea of a woman, akusala cittas did not arise on account of what was seen. However, even the thinking of a woman who smiles can be the object of awareness, and after that enlightenment can be attained if paññā has been developed to that extent. Any kind of reality can be the object of sati and we should not try to select particular objects. If we select particular objects we will not see things as they are, as realities which arise because of their own conditions and which are beyond control, anattā.

The Visuddhimagga (I, 56) continues after the passage about Mahā Tissa with the explanation of the virtue of restraint of the faculties:

> '... if he, if that person, left the eye faculty unguarded, remained with the eye-door unclosed by the door-panel of mindfulness, these states of covetousness, etc. might invade, might pursue, might threaten,

him. He enters upon the way of its restraint: he enters upon the way of closing that eye faculty by the door-panel of mindfulness. It is the same one of whom it is said he guards the eye faculty, undertakes the restraint of the eye faculty.'

This does not mean that we should avoid seeing or hearing, there are conditions for the arising of these realities. If the doorways are unguarded akusala cittas arise on account of what is experienced. We take the object for permanent or for self, we do not know what is really there. When there is, after seeing, hearing or the experiences through the other doors, the development of understanding, the doors are guarded.

With mettā

Nina van Gorkom

Pāli Glossary

Compiled by Jonothan Abbott and Sarah Procter Abbott

abhiññā supernormal power

adhimokkha determination (a cetasika)

adhipati paccaya predominance condition

adosa non-aversion or kindness(a cetasika)

ahetuka rootless (citta)

ahetuka diṭṭhi the wrong view of no cause for what arises

ahirika shamelessness(a cetasika)

ākāsānañcāyatana sphere of boundless space, the subject of the first arūpa jhāna-citta

ākiñcaññāyatana sphere of nothingness, the subject of the third arūpal jhāna-citta

akusala unwholesome

alobha non-attachment or generosity (a cetasika)

amoha understanding (a cetasika)

anāgāmī non-returner, the noble person who has realized the third stage of enlightenment

anantara paccaya proximity condition

anattā non self

anicca impermanent

anottappa recklessness or disregard of unwholesomeness (a cetasika)

anuloma adaptation (citta) arising before jhāna or before enlightenment

anupādisesa nibbāna final nibbāna, khandha parinibbāna at the death of an arahat

anusaya latent tendency

āpo dhātu element of water

appaṇā (samādhi) absorption (concentration)

arahat noble person who has attained the fourth stage of enlightenment

ārammaṇa the object of consciousness

ariya noble, the person who has attained enlightenment

arūpa-brahma-bhūmi plane of existence of immaterial beings. Birth as a result of attaining arūpa jhāna

arūpavacara belonging to the immaterial plane of consciousness, arūpa-jhāna-citta

arūpa-jhāna immaterial absorption

asankhārika strong (cittas) spontaneously arisen, not induced by others

āsava cankers, influxes of intoxicants, group of defilements

asobhana not beautiful, not accompanied by beautiful roots.

asūbha foul

asura demon, being of one of the unhappy planes of existence.

ātāpī heedful, with awareness

atīta bhavanga past life-continuum, arising and falling away shortly before a process of citta experiencing an object through one of the sense-doors starts

āvajjana adverting of consciousness to the object which has impinged on one of the six doors

avijjā ignorance

avyākata dhammas (realities) which are not kusala or akusala

ayoniso manasikāra unwise attention to an object

āyūhana kamma at birth which brings results during a lifetime.

bhāvanā mental development, the development of calm, samatha, and the development of insight, vipassanā.

bhāvanā-māya-paññā understanding based on mental development

bhavanga citta life-continuum citta which does not arise within a process but in between processes

bhavaṅga calana vibrating bhavaṅga, arising shortly before a sense-cognition process starts

bhavaṅgupaccheda arrest bhavaṅga, last bhavaṅga-citta before a process starts. The bhavaṅgupaccheda which arises before a mind-door process is the mind-door of that process.

bhikkhu monk

bhikkhunī nun

bhūmi plane of existence

brahma-vihāra one of the four "divine abidings". which are loving kindness, compassion, sympathetic joy and equanimity

cakkhu eye

cakkhu-dvāra eye-door

cakkhuppasāda rūpa eye-sense

cakkhuviññāṇa seeing-consciousness

cetanā intention or volition (a cetasika)

cetasika mental factor arising with consciousness

chanda interest (a cetasika)

citta consciousness, the chief reality which experiences an object

citta-kammaññatā wieldiness of citta (a cetasika)

citta-lahutā lightness of citta (a cetasika)

citta-mudutā pliancy of citta (a cetasika)

citta-passaddhi tranquility of citta (a cetasika)

citta-pāguññatā proficiency of citta (a cetasika)

citta-ujukatā uprightness of citta (a cetasika)

cuti-citta death consciousness

dāna generosity, giving

dassana kicca function of seeing.

dhamma reality, the natural law, the Teaching of The Buddha

dhammārammaṇa any object which can only be experienced through the mind-door

dhātu element, any reality

diṭṭhi wrong view

diṭṭhigata sampayutta accompanied by wrong view

domanassa unpleasant feeling

dosa aversion or ill-will (a cetasika)

dosa-mūla-citta citta rooted in aversion

dukkha vedanā painful feeling or unpleasant feeling.

dvāra doorway through which an object is experienced, the five sense-doors or the mind-door

dvi-pañca-viññāṇa the five pairs of sense-cognitions, which are seeing, hearing, smelling, tasting and bodily experience

ekaggatā cetasika one-pointedness which makes citta focus on one object.

ghāṇa-dhātu nose element

ghāṇappasāda rūpa nose-sense

ghandha odour

gantha bond, a group of defilements

ghāyana kicca function of smelling

gotrabhū change of lineage citta before jhāna or enlightenment is attained

hadaya-vatthu heart-base

hasituppāda citta smiling-consciousness of the arahat

hetu root

hiri Moral shame (a cetasika)

indriya faculty, leader

issā jealousy, envy (a cetasika)

jāti birth, class (of cittas)

javana impulsion (function of cittas) which "run through" the object

jhāna absorption, burning, developed in samatha or vipassanā

jhāyati it burns

jivhā tongue

jivhāppasāda rūpa tongue base

jīvitindriya life-faculty, (a cetasika or a rūpa)

kalyāṇa mitta good friend

kāma bhūmi sensuous plane of existence

kāmāvacara citta sense-sphere cconsciousness

kamma intention or volition; deed motivated by volition.

kammaṭṭhāna object of samatha bhāvanā

kamma-patha course of action, which is wholesome or unwholesome

karuṇā compassion (a cetasika)

kasiṇa disk, as meditation subject in the development of calm, samatha

kāya collection, body of rūpas or mental body, the cetasikas.

kāya-dhātu body-sense element

kāya-kammaññatā wieldiness of cetasikas (a cetasika)

kāya-lahutā lightness of cetasikas (a cetasika)

kāya-mudutā pliancy of cetasikas (a cetasika)

kāya-pāguññatā proficiency of cetasikas (a cetasika)

kāya-passaddhi tranquility of cetasikas (a cetasika)

kāyappasāda rūpa body-sense

kāya-ujukatā uprightness of cetasikas (a cetasika)

kāyaviññāṇa body consciousness

kāya-viññatti bodily intimation (a rūpa)

khandha one of a group, any conditioned reality, i.e. any rūpa, vedanā, saññā, saṅkhāra or viññāna

kiriya citta inoperative citta which is not kusala, akusala or vipāka

kukkucca Regret, worry (a cetasika)

lakkhaṇa characteristic

lobha attachment (a cetasika)

lobha-mūla-citta citta rooted in attachment

lokiya citta mundane citta

lokuttara citta supramundane citta which experiences nibbāna

lokuttara dhamma nibbāna and a citta or cetasika which experiences nibbāna

macchariya stinginess (a cetasika)

magga path, Eightfold Path

magga-citta path-consciousness, lokuttara citta which experiences nibbāna and eradicates defilements

mahā-bhūta rūpa the rūpa which is one of the four great elements of earth or solidity, water or cohesion, fire or temperature and wind or motion

māna conceit (a cetasika)

manasikāra attention (a cetasika)

mano consciousness, citta

mano-dhātu mind-element. The five-sense-door adverting-consciousness and the two types of receiving consciousness

mano-dvārāvajjana-citta mind-door adverting consciousness

mano-dvāra-vīthi-citta citta arising in a a mind-door process

manoviññāṇa dhātu mind-consciousness element. All cittas other than the sense-cognitions (seeing, etc.) and mind-element cittas

mettā loving kindness

middha torpor (a cetasika)

moha ignorance (a cetasika)

moha-mūla-citta citta rooted in ignorance

muditā sympathetic joy (a cetasika)

nāma any reality which can experience an object

natthika diṭṭhi wrong view that there is no result of kamma

n'eva-saññā-n'āsaññāyatana sphere of neither perception nor non-perception, the object of the fourth immaterial jhāna

nibbāna the unconditioned reality which is freedom from dukkha

nimitta mental image or sign

nirodha-samāpatti attainment of cessation of consciousness

nīvaraṇa hindrance, defilement

ñāṇa wisdom, understanding

oja nutriment (a rūpa)

oḷārika rūpa gross rūpa. Any sense-object or sense-base

ottappa blameless (a cetasika)

paccaya condition

pakatūpanissaya paccaya natural decisive support condition

CHAPTER 11. PĀLI GLOSSARY

pāṇātipāta killing

pañcadvārāvajjana citta five sense-door adverting-consciousness

(dvi-)pañca-viññāṇa citta sense-consciousness (seeing, etc.) There are five pairs

paññā wisdom or understanding

paññatti concept which makes known

paramattha dhamma absolute, ultimate reality

pāramī perfection, 10 pāramī

parikamma citta preparatory consciousness

pariyatti intellectual right understanding of reality

pasāda-rūpa sense-base (eye-sense, ear-sense, nose-sense, tongue-sense, body-sense)

paṭibhāga nimitta counterpart image acquired in the development of calm, samatha

paṭicca samuppāda dependent origination

paṭigha aversion, ill-will, dosa (a cetasika)

Pātimokkha rules for monks

paṭipatti direct understanding of reality, lit. reaching the particular (object)

paṭisandhi citta rebirth consciousness

phala-citta fruit-consciousness which experiences nibbāna as a result of magga citta

phassa contact (a cetasika)

phoṭṭhabbārammaṇa tangible object, experienced through body sense (hardness/softness, heat/cold or motion)

phusana kicca function of experiencing tangible object

pīti joy, (a cetasika)

puthujjana worldling, ordinary person

rasa taste

rūpa physical reality which cannot experience anything.

rūpa-bhūmi plane of beings where birth was the result of rūpa-jhāna, fine-material jhāna

rūpa-brahma-bhūmi fine material plane of existence

rūpa-jhāna fine material absorption

rūpa-khandha any rūpa, one of group of physical phenomena

rūpāvacara citta consciousness of the fine-material sphere, rūpa-jhāna-citta.

sabhāva nature, characteristic of reality

sadda sound

saddhā faith or confidence in wholesomeness

sahetuka accompanied by roots

sakadāgāmī once-returner, noble person who has attained the second stage of enlightenment

samādhi concentration or one-pointedness

samatha calm

sampaṭicchana-citta receiving-consciousness

sampayutta associated with

saṃsāra cycle of births and deaths

saṅkhāra dhamma conditioned reality

saṅkhārakkhandha all cetasikas other than vedanā (feeling) and saññā (memory)

saññā perception or memory

santīraṇa-citta investigating-consciousness

sasaṅkhārika induced by oneself or someone else, weak (citta)

sassatavāda diṭṭhi eternalist view

sati awareness (a cetasika)

satipaṭṭhāna awareness of a reality. It can be the cetasika sati or the object of mindfulness

sa-upādi-sesa nibbāna arahatship with the khandhas or "groups of existing" remaining

sīla morality, behaviour of cittas

sīlabbatupādāna wrong practice which is clinging to certain rules (rites and rituals)

sobhaṇa beautiful, accompanied by beautiful roots

somanassa pleasant feeling.

sota-dhātu element of ear.

sota-dvāra-vīthi ear-door process

sotāpanna noble person who has attained the first stage of enlightenment

sota viññāṇa hearing-consciousness

sukha-vedanā pleasant feeling

tadālambana/tadārammaṇa retention or registering, last citta of a complete process.

Tathāgata "Thus-gone", The Buddha

tatramajjhattatā equanimity or even-mindedness (a cetasika)

tejo dhātu element of fire or heat.

thīna sloth (a cetasika)

uddhacca restlessness (a cetasika)

upacāra access or proximity (concentration)

upādā rūpa derived rūpa, any rūpa other than the four great elements

upādāna clinging

upādānakkhandha any khandha which is the object of clinging.

upekkhā indifferent feeling or equanimity

vacī-viññatti speech intimation (a rūpa)

vatthu base, physical base of citta.

vāyo dhātu element of wind or motion.

vedanā feeling (a cetasika)

vicāra sustained thought.

vicikicchā doubt (a cetasika)

CHAPTER 11. PĀLI GLOSSARY

vinaya discipline for monks

viññāṇa consciousness

viññāṇa khandha aggregate of consciousness, any citta

viññāṇañcāyatana sphere of boundless consciousness, subject for the second stage of immaterial jhāna

vipāka citta (and cetasikas) which are the result of kamma.

vipallāsa perversion

vipassanā insight, wisdom which sees realities as they are.

vippayutta unaccompanied by.

viriya energy, effort, patience (a cetasika)

vitakka striking, directs the citta to the object (a cetasika)

vīthicitta citta arising in a process

vīthi-vimutti-citta process freed citta, citta which does not arise within a process.

voṭṭhapana determining consciousness

vyāpāda ill-will

yoniso manasikāra wise attention

12

Books by Nina van Gorkom

- *The Buddha's Path*. An Introduction to the doctrine of Theravada Buddhism for those who have no previous knowledge. The four noble Truths - suffering - the origin of suffering - the cessation of suffering - and the way leading to the end of suffering - are explained as a philosophy and a practical guide which can be followed in today's world.

- *Buddhism in Daily Life*. A general introduction to the main ideas of Theravada Buddhism. The purpose of this book is to help the reader gain insight into the Buddhist scriptures and the way in which the teachings can be used to benefit both ourselves and others in everyday life.

- *Abhidhamma in Daily Life* is an exposition of absolute realities in detail. Abhidhamma means higher doctrine and the book's purpose is to encourage the right application of Buddhism in order to eradicate wrong view and eventually all defilements.

- *Cetasikas.* Cetasika means 'belonging to the mind'. It is a mental factor which accompanies consciousness (citta) and experiences an object. There are 52 cetasikas. This book gives an outline of each of these 52 cetasikas and shows the relationship they have with each other.

- *The Buddhist Teaching on Physical Phenomena.* A general introduction to physical phenomena and the way they are related to each other and to mental phenomena. The purpose of this book is to show that the study of both mental phenomena and physical phenomena is indispensable for the development of the eightfold Path.

- *The Conditionality of Life.* This book is an introduction to the seventh book of the Abhidhamma, that deals with the conditionality of life. It explains the deep underlying motives for all actions through body, speech and mind and shows that these are dependent on conditions and cannot be controlled by a 'self'. This book is suitable for those who have already made a study of the Buddha's teachings.

- *Letters on Vipassanā.* This book consists of a compilation of letters on the Dhamma to Sarah Abbott, Alan Weller, Robert Kirkpatrick and other friends. The material used are tapes of Khun Sujin's lectures and conversations with her on the development of right understanding. She encourages people to develop the understanding of the present moment, since that is the way to the ultimate goal, namely, the eradication of the clinging to the concept of self and of all other defilements.

- *A Survey of Paramattha Dhammas* by Sujin Boriharnwanaket, translated by Nina van Gorkom. A Survey of Paramattha Dhammas is a guide to the development of the Buddha's path of wisdom, covering all aspects of human life and human behaviour, good and bad. This study explains that right understanding is indispensable for mental development, the development of calm as well as the development of insight.

- *The Perfections Leading to Enlightenment* by Sujin Boriharnwanaket, translated by Nina van Gorkom. The Perfections is a study of the ten good qualities: generosity, morality, renunciation, wisdom, energy, patience, truthfulness, determination, loving-kindness, and equanimity.

- *An Introduction to the Buddhist scriptures* with the aim to encourage the reader to study the texts themselves. In that way they can verify that the Buddha's words were directed to the practice of what he taught, in particular to the development of right understanding of all phenomena of life.

- *Understanding Realities Now: Nina's Travelogues.* Compilation of articles discussing the development of insight, the understanding of the present moment in daily life. It contains over 60 quotes from the original scriptures and commentaries.

- *Buddhism: Learning to understand life.* The purpose of this book is to help the reader gain insight into how Buddhism works to understand life. It is not mere theory, but it is to be applied right now, at this moment. The Buddha taught that all mental phenomena and physical phenomena which naturally appear in our daily life can be objects of mindfulness and right understanding. Available on Amazon Kindle only.

- *Undertanding Life Now*, authors Sarah Procter Abbott and Nina van Gorkom. The beginning of the Buddha's Path is the understanding of life now, little by little. The Teachings of the Buddha are unique in revealing that each conditioned reality in life is not only impermanent and unsatisfactory but also anattā, not-self. This book consists of 276 Jottings taken from Zoom discussions during the Covid-19 pandemic.

www.ingramcontent.com/pod-product-compliance
Lightning Source LLC
Chambersburg PA
CBHW022117040426
42450CB00006B/740